Support Groups for Older People
Who Have Been Abused

Violence and Abuse Series

This new series forms a set of accessible books for practitioners, managers and policy makers working in social and health care, probation and criminology. Each book draws on a key piece of research or current practice relating to violence and abuse to give practical guidance on new ways of working with both victims and perpetrators to bring about positive change.

also in the series

Male Victims of Elder Abuse
Their Experiences and Needs
Jacki Pritchard
ISBN 1 85302 999 8

of related interest

Training Manual for Working with Older People in Residential and Day Care
Jacki Pritchard
ISBN 1 84310 123 8

Elder Abuse Work
Best Practice in Britain and Canada
Edited by Jacki Pritchard
ISBN 1 85302 704 9

Good Practice with Vulnerable Adults
Edited by Jacki Pritchard
ISBN 1 85302 982 3
Good Practice in Social Work 9

The Essential Groupworker
Teaching and Learning Creative Groupwork
Mark Doel and Catherine Sawdon
ISBN 1 85302 823 1

Groupwork in Social Care
Planning and Setting Up Groups
Julie Phillips
ISBN 1 85302 829 0

The Care Homes Legal Handbook
Jeremy Cooper
ISBN 1 84310 064 9

Counselling Adult Survivors of Child Sexual Abuse
Christiane Sanderson
ISBN 1 85302 138 5

Support Groups for Older People Who Have Been Abused

Beyond Existing

Jacki Pritchard

Jessica Kingsley Publishers
London and New York

The right of Jacki Pritchard to be identified as author of this work has been asserted by her in accordance with the Copyright, Designs and Patents Act 1988.

First published in the United Kingdom in 2003
by Jessica Kingsley Publishers Ltd
116 Pentonville Road
London N1 9JB, England
and
29 West 35th Street, 10th fl.
New York, NY 10001-2299

www.jkp.com

Copyright © 2003 Jacki Pritchard

Library of Congress Cataloging in Publication Data

Pritchard, Jacki.
    Support groups for older people who have been abused : Beyond Existing/ Jacki Pritchard.
    p. cm.
    Includes bibliographical references and index.
    ISBN 1-84310-102-5 (pbk. : alk. Paper)
    1. Aged--Abuse of--Prevention. 2. Social work with the aged. 3. Abused aged. 4. Social work with the aged--Great Britain. 5. Beyond Existing (Project) I. Title.

HV6626.3 .P76 2003
362.6--dc21

                                                                    2002038914

British Library Cataloguing in Publication Data
A CIP catalogue record for this book is available from the British Library

ISBN 1 84310 102 5

Printed and Bound in Great Britain by
Athenaeum Press, Gateshead, Tyne and Wear

Contents

This book is dedicated to the members of
Beyond Existing, without whom
the book could not have been written.

Acknowledgements

It is of paramount importance to protect the victims who participated in this project. It was a major objective whilst the project was running, but also when writing up the findings. The victims agreed that information could be written up in this book with the proviso their anonymity would be respected. I want to thank them for being involved and for their openness and honesty, from which I have learnt so much and I hope will be of value to others.

Because of the need to maintain anonymity, I cannot name the people and local organisations who supported Beyond Existing, but they know who they are and I wish to express my gratitude to them. Beyond Existing could not have survived without the support of Churchtown Social Services Department; in particular the managers of the Quarry and Calder Centres. Special thanks are due to Rachel, my co-leader, who has been there throughout the good and bad times and who has made me laugh when I needed to!

In the book I explain about the difficulty of securing funding for the project, so I am indebted to the following organisations who did support us financially:

- The Joseph Rowntree Foundation
- Churchtown Coalfield Partnership Community Chest Fund
- Churchtown Health Action Zone
- The Esmée Fairbairn Foundation
- The Nationwide Foundation

Finally, I need to say another big 'thank-you' to Eric Sainsbury, who was involved in the original research project; he has supported me again throughout this project and commented on the various drafts of this book.

Note

The Joseph Rowntree Foundation has supported this project as part of its programme of research and innovative development projects, which it hopes will be of value to policy makers and practitioners. The facts presented and views expressed in this book are, however, those of the author and not necessarily those of the Foundation.

Terminology used in the book

Abuse
This includes physical, sexual, psychological, financial, neglect, discriminatory.

Adult abuse
Any form of abuse which has happened when a person has been an adult, i.e. over 18 years of age.

Centres
Establishments which have residential and day care facilities.

Domestic violence
Physical, emotional, sexual violence experienced by either a woman or a man.

Elder abuse
Any form of abuse which has happened to a person over the age of 65 years.

Groups
Set up by Beyond Existing between June 2000 and June 2002 and shall be referred to as Quarry, Calder and Morrison.

Leader
Person who works with members and facilitates the sessions.

Member
Victim who attended one of the groups.

Session
Group meeting.

Victim
Someone who has experienced abuse, whether it be physical, sexual, emotional, financial, neglect, discriminatory.

CHAPTER 1

The Project
Beyond Existing

Introduction

There are plenty of sources about groupwork per se, but little detailed work has been written about how support groups can help older people. This book's objective is to give an account of how an organisation called Beyond Existing was set up specifically to support older people who had been victims of abuse, either earlier in their lives or later in life. I shall conclude that such support groups potentially offer a beneficial way in which to help victims heal, and from the information given about the work which was undertaken I hope that other workers will be encouraged to work in similar ways. Before explaining how Beyond Existing came into existence, it may be useful to consider the definition and purposes of groupwork.

Groupwork

All sorts of groups are formed in everyday life; some groups come together naturally (e.g. family), others are forced together (e.g. at work or in a social situation), others may come together for a specific purpose (e.g. a political group, pressure group). In many organisations within all the sectors (statutory, voluntary and private) groups are formed as a way of helping a collection of individuals with a specific problem; over the years this has become known as groupwork, and as such 'is a professional tool in a range of human service agencies' (Phillips 2001, p.9).

The history of groupwork goes back many years and a useful overview of social groupwork can be found in Konopka (1983). Groupwork has been one method of working for social workers since before the 1960s (Davies 1975; McCullough and Ely 1969), but over the past forty years the theory and development in this field have become more sophisticated. Groupwork was well established in North America long before it became popular in the UK. During the 1970s and 1980s this way of working became more common in various fields of social care. Brown says this was:

> ...partly due to the North American influence, but more likely due to the push for diversification and improvement of practice intervention methods. This arose in part from the discouraging research evaluations of the efficacy of traditional one-to-one casework methods. (Brown 1994, p.1)

In the new millennium, groupwork may have a more prominent part to play, as individual social workers are overburdened with heavy caseloads and often do not have the time to undertake the necessary long-term work with service users. It is possible for workers from any discipline to develop skills to become a groupworker. When there is such great emphasis on *working in partnership,* it would be timely to encourage workers from different agencies to work together to lead groups. Workers functioning in different roles could work successfully to provide many types of groups to meet various needs of service users. It can be argued that in a time when resources are tight, groupwork is a more cost-effective way of working.

This is a forceful argument when in the adult sector social workers frequently complain they are 'number-crunching'; that is, managers expect them to get through as many assessments as possible and long-term work is not common practice. It is likely in the future that other professionals and care workers will undertake the long-term work with service users, and groupwork may be one method of working which could be promoted.

It is necessary to briefly consider the role of groupwork generally in social work practice. Doel and Sawdon (1999, p.18) ask the questions, 'When we survey the state of social work practice, where is groupwork? What presence does it have? In short, how much groupwork is there?' They conclude, 'The best guess is that groupwork's presence is patchy' (p.19). Nevertheless, there is a vast amount of literature on groupwork, and traditional texts are now in their second or third editions (e.g. Brown 1994; Douglas 2000).

Defining groupwork

So what is groupwork? There has been much debate about this and Phillips concludes that many of the written works are 'of little utility to the reader', because 'their definitions usually try to encompass all forms of human groups from the family to specific, time-limited treatment groups' (Phillips 2001, p.17). It is true that there can be many different 'types' of group, which may have equally as many purposes. For example, to illustrate diversity within social care, there may be groups run for relatives who are carers; residents in care homes; children who have been sexually abused. Some groups are concerned with social functioning, others with therapy. Workers from different disciplines may be involved in running groups – social workers, psychotherapists, residential/day care workers, support workers, volunteers. Hence the term 'groupwork' can be very broad. Common purposes may be to help people with a problem(s), to resolve the problem and to facilitate change. One of the most frequently quoted definitions comes from Konopka in the 1980s:

> Social groupwork is a method of social work which helps individuals to enhance their social functioning through purposeful group experiences, and to cope more effectively with their personal, group or community problems. (Konopka 1983, p.18)

Later in the 1980s, Shulman (1988) described groupwork as 'a laboratory for learning'. Heap is another established theorist on groupwork, who says that groupwork 'often increases the quality and the relevance of help' as well as offering the capacity 'to help as well as be helped' (Heap 1979, 1985). This definition emphasises helping the individual with a problem. A more recent definition from Brown adds:

> ...groupwork provides a context in which *individuals help each other*; it is a method of *helping groups* as well as helping individuals; and it can enable individuals and groups to *influence* and *change* personal, group, organisational and community problems. (Brown 1994, p.8)

Gillies and James divided groups into psyche and socio:

> **Psyche** groups exist to provide emotional satisfaction for their members and they tend to be informal, for example, the women who always sit together in the small lounge in a residential home, in order to be together. **Socio** groups come together to pursue specific goals, for example a reminiscence group. (Gillies and James 1994, p.36)

All these definitions are relevant to the work which is undertaken in the Beyond Existing groups.

Aims of groupwork

A group has to have a purpose. Questions which have to be asked are – Why are people coming together? What do they hope to achieve? Whose group is it? Who 'owns' it? Douglas states:

> It is essential that the purpose for which a group is established should be clear – at least, as clear as it is possible to be, given the circumstances in which the convenor finds him/herself. This helps to make the establishment of any kind of group a very logical process. (Douglas 2000, p.71)

Brown lists possible groupwork aims as:

- individual assessment
- individual support and maintenance
- individual change
- educational, information-giving and training groups
- leisure/compensatory
- mediation between individuals and social systems
- group change and/or support
- environmental change
- social change.

(Summarised from Brown 1994, pp.10–13)

Beyond Existing had *overt* aims; that is, they were disclosed and made clear at the outset. This will be discussed further in the following chapters.

Older people and groupwork

In many aspects of life, older people are not given the same attention as children or younger adults. This is true when one looks for studies of groupwork with older people. It is possible to find short articles or chapters referring to work with people in residential and day care settings (e.g. Bernard *et al.* 1988; Burton 1989; Lewis 1992; Mullender 1990; Mullender and Ward 1991). Much of the useful literature is to be found in the journal *Groupwork*. However, the number of larger works is minimal compared to all the studies which have been undertaken with other service user groups (e.g. adolescents, sex offenders, people with mental health problems). Nevertheless, there are some very useful texts about groupwork with older people – one being Paula Crimmens' *Storymaking and Creative Groupwork with Older People*. Crimmens argues:

> There are many good reasons for organising a group...
> In the move away from the medical model of caring for a
> person's physical needs towards a more holistic and person-centred approach which includes emotional and social needs, activities offer all kinds of opportunities.
>
> Here are some of the aims:
>
> - contact and relationship building
> - providing an experience of community for people who may be feeling very isolated
> - enjoyment

- self-esteem

- a reduction in boredom and an increase in interest

- providing an ideal opportunity for the practice of the person-centred approach

- maintaining and extending people's physical and mental abilities.

(Crimmens 1998, pp.15–16)

There are numerous texts on survivors of child abuse and domestic violence, but little has been written about older people as survivors (Pritchard 2000, 2001). Yet the value of groupwork with survivors is widely recognised:

> Being with other survivors is a critical part of the healing process, and joining a group is an ideal way to work with other women who've been abused. Groupwork is particularly useful for dealing with shame, isolation and secrecy. If you're still fuzzy about what happened to you, hearing other women's stories can stimulate your memories. Their words can loosen buried feelings. Talking with other survivors is useful for problem-solving, also. There's likely to be at least one other woman in the room who has suggestions for dealing with whatever issue you're facing. (Bass and Davis 1988, p.462)

Yet another omission in research is groupwork undertaken with older men who have been abused. Most people tend to think of female survivors rather than male survivors who may have experienced abuse in childhood or later in life. So there is clearly a need to address these gaps in research. Beyond Existing may be one project which contributes to increasing our knowledge in this field.

How Beyond Existing started

Beyond Existing came into being as a follow-on project to a research project entitled *The Needs of Older Women: Services for Victims of Elder Abuse and Other Abuse* (Pritchard 2000), which had been funded by the Joseph Rowntree Foundation between 1997 and 1999. The aim was to test out whether support groups could be one way of meeting the needs of older people who had been abused. The purpose of this book is to present the findings of this second project. However, it will be helpful to give the reader some background information about the original project before presenting the findings.

The original project

The original project was carried out in three social services departments located in the North of England. Fictitious names have been adopted for these:

- Churchtown

- Millfield

- Tallyborough.

The main aims of the project were to:

1.   identify women who were victims of elder abuse

2.   carry out a small study to identify the extent to which victims of elder abuse have also experienced abuse earlier in their lives

3.   identify the types of abuse experienced (in childhood and adulthood)

4.   identify the needs of victims

5.   consider what resources/services should be
      provided for victims.

In order to identify the needs of women who had been abused,
both quantitative and qualitative research methods were used.
The methods adopted for the research project needed to fulfil
two main objectives:

1.   To collect quantitative data regarding the victims,
      their abusers and the types of abuse suffered.

2.   To collect qualitative data about victims'
      experiences of abuse and to identify need, both for
      protection and in coming to terms with their
      abusive experiences.

For a full explanation of the methods used the reader should
refer to the original research report (Pritchard 2000); data were
collected by means of:

- monitoring forms and questionnaires
- focus groups/talks
- in-depth interviews
- telephone interviews with workers
- case files, case conference minutes, and individual
  protection plans.

Focus groups were run for older women in a variety of settings
to discuss the issues and problems associated with abuse and
also to identify women who could participate in in-depth interviews with the researcher. While the focus groups were
running, older men regularly started asking the researcher if
they could attend the groups. They were allowed to do so when
the women had no objections to their participation. In all,

more than 300 older people took part in the groups. Both women and men talked freely in the groups about the abuse they had experienced, but male victims also approached the researcher to ask for time to talk privately about their experiences and needs. Consequently, the focus of enquiry broadened to include men in the study, and their contribution and circumstances were written up separately from the final report on women (Pritchard 2001).

Definition of abuse

Many definitions of elder abuse exist and can be open to interpretation. For the purposes of the research project, the following definition was adopted:

> Abuse may be described as physical, sexual, psychological or financial. It may be intentional or unintentional or the result of neglect. It causes harm to the older person, either temporarily or over a period of time. (Department of Health 1993, p.3)

This definition was used in conjunction with the adult abuse policies and procedures already established in Churchtown and Millfield and a working document which existed in Tallyborough.

Needs identified

When in-depth interviews were conducted with 39 victims of elder abuse, both female and male victims were clear about their needs relating to the past and the present abuse; these are summarised in Tables 1.1 and 1.2.

Table 1.1 Summary of needs as identified by female victims
• advice
• choice/options
• companionship
• control over own life/own affairs
• counselling
• feeling able to trust other people
• food and warmth
• health
• hobbies/interests
• housing
• information
• money/benefits/pension
• people (helpers of various kinds)
• physical help
• place of safety
• practical help
• privacy
• telephone numbers of possible helpers
• the support of religious beliefs

- to be believed
- to be listened to
- to be safe
- to feel safe in the house/community
- to forget what has happened
- to get out and about
- to know who to go to for help
- to leave the abusive situation
- to protect the family/abuser
- to reduce the fear of crime
- to stop the abuse/violence
- to talk

from Joseph Rowntree Foundation, May 2000, p.2;
Pritchard 2000, p.74

Table 1.2 Summary of needs as identified by male victims

- advice
- assessment of medical problems
- assessment of mental capacity
- company
- maintaining contact with social worker
- management of finances
- permission to talk
- personal safety
- physical/basic care
- place of safety
- police involvement
- practical help
- protection of the abuser
- reconciliation with family
- rehousing/permanent accommodation
- remain loyal and do one's duty
- talk about abuse
- talk about/deal with losses

from Pritchard 2001, p.59

What they expressed very clearly was that their main need was to talk about the abuse they had experienced. Those victims who had been abused in childhood had rarely told anybody about what had happened to them; similarly, victims of domestic violence had held the common belief that it was only happening to them. Older people have lived in an era when they were expected to keep things to themselves, it was not usual for them to vent their feelings as people are encouraged to do today. However, giving 'permission to speak' (that is, the knowledge that they could talk to someone and be listened to) facilitated disclosure about abuse which had happened not only recently but earlier in life. There was an urgent kind of recognition among victims themselves that their stories had to be told before they died; some victims only needed to tell their story once, others needed ongoing help and support.

At the end of the project, focus groups were run for some of the interviewees and questionnaires were sent out to others in order to validate the findings. At the end of these focus groups victims said they had found it helpful to meet with other people who had also experienced abuse, and would like to continue to do this in the future. In the event, even more disclosures came out during these groups:

> It was particularly interesting that all the women set about the tasks of discussing the project's findings and succeeded in giving very valuable comments, but they also (with the exception of Florence) started to tell their stories again to each other – and said they found it helpful to talk to women who had similar experiences to themselves. (Pritchard 2000, p.106)

The final report concluded:

The lessons for peer support groups learnt from this group experience have been:

- Victims should be encouraged to attend peer support groups even if the idea is alien to them in the first instance.

- Victims might be more willing to attend if they can bring a support person with them (Joan wanted her social worker with her throughout the group; Vera just wanted someone to bring her to the door).

- Victims may get something positive from hearing other victims' stories.

- Consideration should be given to the types of abuse experienced and its possible effects on other participants. (Pritchard 2000, p.106)

This was how Beyond Existing began to evolve. It was these comments from the focus groups, together with the identified need to talk, that suggested that support groups could be run in such a way as to be both supportive and therapeutic.

The original project had highlighted the fact that practical and emotional support was needed both for victims who were still living in abusive situations, and also for victims who had left them. Very often, outstanding practical problems had not been resolved and victims continued to need advice and information regarding benefits, finances, housing and legal matters. The findings indicated that little long-term supportive or therapeutic work was undertaken with victims once the immediate crisis had been resolved. Little thought was put into addressing such long-term needs as meeting the physical and psychological effects of abuse. Older victims were rarely given the opportunity to heal:

> There needs to be recognition that victims may need ongoing help and support for a long period of time... There are many stages of healing – as there are for younger victims of abuse. Recognition that this can take years rather than months is crucial in planning resources for future intervention. Few victims had been offered the opportunity to work through their ongoing problems or their feelings about the abuse they had experienced. (Pritchard 2000, p.7)

It was with this in mind that Beyond Existing was set up to undertake long-term work with both female and male victims.

The Joseph Rowntree Foundation agreed to fund a pilot project which ran for six months from June 2000 (and became known as Stage 1). The pilot study set up two groups which were quite different in composition. One was for women only, all of whom were mentally sound. The other one was for men and women, who had different levels of mental capacity. Both groups continued to run after the pilot study had concluded and met between January and June 2001, which became known as Stage 2.

Stage 3 saw the setting up of a new group which was very different in composition to the previous groups: it included younger adults (ages ranging from 39 to 56 years) who had mental health problems, and one member had learning disabilities. All these adults were referred by social workers. The findings of this stage are included in this book because it will be shown how younger and older adults can work with and support each other successfully. (All these stages are summarised in Table 1.3.)

Table 1.3 Summary of stages
Stage 1: Pilot study which ran from June to December 2000. Two groups were set up, which shall be known as Quarry and Calder. Quarry was a mixed group. Calder was an all-women group.
Stage 2: Quarry and Calder groups continued until June 2001.
Stage 3: New group set up October 2002 – current. The group will be known as Morrison. This was an all-women group, which included younger and older adults with mental health problems and learning disabilities.

An objective of Beyond Existing has been to test out different ways of working in groups. The findings of this project will be presented by discussing all three stages, and their successes and failures, and drawing conclusions in the final chapter.

What follows is a report about how the groups were set up and the work which was undertaken; it will be an honest account of the difficulties and struggles we encountered, but also the benefits which were reaped. Mention will also be made of another area of work which emerged – responding to telephone enquiries and giving advice to victims, members of the public and home care staff who wanted to report abuse, and residential workers who had concerns about practices in their workplaces.

Anonymity

All the names in the book have been changed to protect the victims and also the workers involved. The geographical areas and groups have also been given fictitious names.

CHAPTER 2

Setting Up the Groups

This chapter will explain how the groups associated with Beyond Existing came into existence. A great deal of work had to take place before the groups could start. This chapter should give potential leaders an insight into what needs to be done and just how much work has to be undertaken both on a practical and emotional level.

Why the name?

Why did we call the groups Beyond Existing? The name came up naturally during a conversation I was having with my co-leader, Rachel. We were talking about how victims do survive by getting on with their lives and developing their own coping strategies. A comment was made, 'But they often feel that they just exist; they're not really living.' It occurred to us that we wanted to help victims by taking them beyond this existence and hence came 'Beyond Existing'.

Why the logo?

Beyond Existing's logo (shown above) depicts the way we wanted to help victims of abuse. We wanted to strive to take them over the rainbow from the rain to the sunshine. We knew through the group sessions that there would be times when the victims would feel sad and when they would feel happy.

The beginning

As discussed in Chapter 1, over the past twenty years a substantial amount of literature has developed on 'groupwork' and how to run successful groups. I wanted to run two support groups in order to test out different ways of working with older people who had been abused. Churchtown Social Services Department was very welcoming of the idea and offered to help in any way they could. Below we shall see how they supported this work in a practical sense. The short-term objective was to run a pilot study for a six-month period in two centres, which shall be known as Quarry and Calder (their differences are noted in Table 2.1).

Table 2.1 Differences between the two groups

Quarry Group	Calder Group
• two group leaders	• one group leader
• male and female victims	• female victims only
• mixed levels of mental capacity	• all mentally capacitated
• met in the morning	• met in the afternoon

Advisory group

The Joseph Rowntree Foundation agreed to fund the meetings of an advisory group which would monitor and evaluate the activities of Beyond Existing. The advisory group included the following professionals:

- administrator
- barrister
- community psychologist
- day care co-ordinator
- manager of a respite/day care unit, who was also an approved social worker
- police inspector
- probation officer
- psychotherapist
- social worker

- research manager

- university professor.

Before the groups started a set of rules was developed, as shown below.

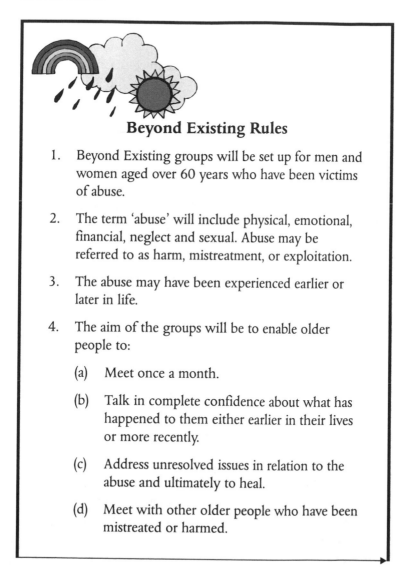

Beyond Existing Rules

1. Beyond Existing groups will be set up for men and women aged over 60 years who have been victims of abuse.

2. The term 'abuse' will include physical, emotional, financial, neglect and sexual. Abuse may be referred to as harm, mistreatment, or exploitation.

3. The abuse may have been experienced earlier or later in life.

4. The aim of the groups will be to enable older people to:

   (a) Meet once a month.

   (b) Talk in complete confidence about what has happened to them either earlier in their lives or more recently.

   (c) Address unresolved issues in relation to the abuse and ultimately to heal.

   (d) Meet with other older people who have been mistreated or harmed.

> (e)   Have support from other older people who have had similar experiences.
>
> (f)   Obtain advice if required.
>
> 5.   The groups will be led by an independent consultant who specialises in working with abuse, risk assessment and violence.
>
> 6.   There will be an Advisory Group consisting of people who have expertise in the field to monitor the activities of the groups.

After the groups had been running for a while and it seemed that members were benefiting from the work, it was decided that grant applications needed to be made to secure funding so that the groups could continue. It was at this point that a mission statement was developed:

Mission statement

To provide long-term counselling, support and skilled help to older victims (both men and women) of physical, emotional, sexual and financial abuse, mistreatment and harm in the area of Churchtown; many of whom are likely to be living in abusive conditions, too frightened or afraid to leave them behind or to take active steps to improve their situation without sympathetic professional support and counselling aimed at demonstrating that older victims do not need to tolerate abuse and that they can improve their lives free from fear, no matter how old they may be.

Practical matters

Group leaders

The Quarry Group was run by me and Rachel, the Day Centre Co-ordinator at the Quarry Centre. The Calder Group was run by me.

Issue of gender

When setting up a group the gender of the leaders needs to be considered. This can be an important issue when dealing with victims who have been sexually abused. If it is an open group and new members come in, sometimes nothing can then be done regarding the leadership of the group, particularly in respect of gender. This is one reason why it is important to screen people before they attend a group. Three women had been sexually abused (Beatrice, Lilian and Vera) and this was known before the groups started. Two men joined the groups later on, both of whom had been sexually abused. William had been raped by a man; for him talking to a female was not problematic. Jim had been abused by his wife but said he was nonetheless happy to work with women. One can never assume that if a person has been abused by one gender they would prefer to work with someone of the opposite gender. It is better to ask!

History of abuse

It is often argued that one of the leaders should be a survivor in order to accelerate feelings of mutual trust among group members (Gordy 1983). I totally agree with this, but have to add the proviso that the person must have worked through their own issues. A danger can be that, once the work is being undertaken, that leader-survivor may be engaging in the group for the wrong reasons. Hall and Lloyd (1989), writing about incest survivors' groups, state:

It is our view that one of the facilitators should not have suffered sexual abuse. This enables the group to be provided with a yardstick of more 'normal' childhood experiences and enables the facilitators to acknowledge the pain of individual group members without triggering off their own pain. (Hall and Lloyd 1989, p.145)

Venues

Two of the centres in Churchtown had been actively involved in the original research project and both managers were very enthusiastic about developing the support groups within their centres. The social services department fully supported this work, so the venues and refreshments were given as donations in kind. When choosing a venue to run a group, leaders should give thought to a number of things which are summarised below.

Table 2.2 Important considerations when choosing a venue
• privacy
• safety
• comfortable room
• equipment
• easy access to toilets
• smoking facilities
• refreshments

Privacy and safety

The safety of a victim of abuse is of paramount importance. Older people may have lived in the same community all their lives. A concern for them is that other people using the venue may see them and want to know why they are coming into the building. Therefore, it is vital that privacy can be maintained and this will be discussed further in the next chapter.

Some victims attending the group may still be living in the abusive situation or may need to have their whereabouts kept confidential. The leaders need to consider safety issues before the groups begin. Will the victim be safe when coming to the group?

Vera attended the Calder Group, which was located in the village where her husband lived. She was offered the alternative of attending the Quarry Group but chose not to do so. It was important to arrive at an agreement that her social worker or a colleague from the same social work team would bring Vera to the door of the venue and make sure she entered safely. In the event, no difficulties arose regarding her arrival to meetings.

However, it is also important that other staff take responsibility for giving the correct information. On one occasion, the minibus driver who was taking Vera home was given her previous address (where her husband still resided) by the secretary in the hospital social work department. For some reason the driver assumed that Vera was confused when she said her address was elsewhere. Fortunately, he checked with me before leaving and we realised that he had been given the wrong information. In fact, Vera was perfectly mentally sound. Thus, it was also important to raise the issue of stereotyping with the driver; he had automatically assumed that Vera was confused when she started to challenge the information he had been given. It was probably due to the fact that he transports many confused people during his working week, but this does not justify stereotyping all older people who visit a centre.

The room

The environment is important to group members. It is not helpful if a room is dark and gloomy; it needs to be well lit and pleasantly furnished, so that people can feel comfortable and relaxed. Some older people may have conditions which necessitate certain kinds of seating. For example, someone with a bad back will not want to sit in a low chair. If a room is being donated free of charge, it is important to check it out before accepting the offer. (Table 2.3 summarises the main considerations when choosing a room.)

Table 2.3 Important considerations when choosing a room
• Privacy – is there a glass door/windows into the room?
• The size of the room – is there enough space, taking into account that personal space may be very important to a victim, especially to those who have been sexually abused? Also there may be a need for a victim to work privately with a group leader during a session.
• The number of chairs available.
• What sort of chairs they are – height, soft, hard.
• The availability of tables – to put drinks on, or larger tables if working in pairs, trios.
• The location of sockets – if using TV/video equipment.
• The room's location in relation to toilets.

Equipment

Leaders may wish to use certain equipment during group sessions, e.g. video, flipchart paper and stand. Again, prior to using a venue, the leaders need to find out whether the equipment is available to use or whether they will have to bring things with them.

Toilets

The location of toilets near to the meeting room is another consideration. If any group members have mobility problems they will not want to walk far because that may mean that they will have to leave the session for a lengthy period of time.

Ground rules need to take into account that people can leave the room to go to the toilet at any time, but the timing of breaks should also be stipulated so that members know in advance how long they might have to wait. Some victims may have continence problems. Group leaders should ensure that they have access to or make available continence pads, spare clothing.

Smoking facilities

Many venues are no-smoking buildings. Fortunately, in the venues used by Beyond Existing there were smoking rooms. If a victim is a smoker they may need to have a cigarette when they become distressed. The group should reach agreement about smoking and, as indicated above, about taking regular breaks.

Refreshments

Beyond Existing was fortunate in that Churchtown Social Services provided drinks free of charge. The manager of the Quarry Centre offered members of the Quarry Group the opportunity to stay for lunch after the session, which they all accepted. If that had not been the case the leaders would have had to secure funding to provide the refreshments and also, maybe, to provide their own crockery and cutlery. It should be remembered that not everyone likes to drink tea or coffee. If a member has a preference for something else this should be made known. One of the things that came out during the first session with Beatrice when undertaking some reminiscence work was that she loved ginger beer. So for the next session she was given a bottle which she could take back to the residential home. Lilian loved sweets, so these were also provided. Providing these things made the women feel more relaxed, and it also showed they were being listened to.

The provision of food became an issue during the running of the groups. On occasions members would arrive not having had any breakfast. Reasons for this varied: a member may not have been fed in the residential home; or was being neglected by a family member; or felt depressed and only felt like eating when s/he got to the group. During Stage 3 the timing of the sessions had to change sometimes, so that sessions happened over lunchtime. It was important to provide food during the meeting.

Transport

Initially it had been thought that social workers would transport the members to the groups in order to save on costs. This proved to be problematic for several reasons. Some members no longer had a social worker involved; some social workers said they 'did not have the time' to do this; it was not seen as a priority. One social worker actually complained that it had taken 'an hour out of my day to get him here and there is a pile of paperwork waiting on my desk. I can't do this again.' So alternative arrangements had to be made.

Not all social workers had the same attitude. For some members it was very important to be transported by someone they knew and trusted. In all three stages both group leaders became involved in transporting some of the victims; others were happy to come in a taxi which was booked for them. Because the Calder Group took place later in the afternoon, the manager of the centre offered the use of a minibus to transport members to and from the sessions.

Regularity of meetings

Many survivor groups meet weekly for a previously set period of time. There were a lot of practical reasons why this could not happen for the pilot study. Therefore, it was decided that initially the groups would plan to meet once a month and the participants would be asked about the frequency once the groups were up and running (see Chapter 10 on evaluation).

Books often advocate what should happen in an ideal world, but in the real world many outside factors can affect what you would like to do. This was the case when arranging the sessions for the groups. We had to think about frequency, timing and duration.

Many of our decisions were made as a direct result of constraints on our resources. People involved with Beyond Existing were giving their time voluntarily (or were being allowed to become involved during work-time, which had its own constraints). The frequency of the meetings was determined by these factors. The groups met monthly, which may not have been ideal for survivor groups. It is often argued that such groups should meet more frequently to keep up the momentum and facilitate regular attendance: preference tends to be given to the idea of a weekly commitment, particularly when changes of attitude are an objective. Another important consideration is that a survivor should not be left too long to dwell on painful issues which have been raised during the session. To offset this potential problem, arrangements were made to follow up victims individually after each session and to arrange visits during the intervening month if necessary.

Timing and duration

Timing had to be fitted around when the rooms were available in the centres. The manager of the Calder Centre had offered the minibus to be used for transport purposes so this had to fit in with the commitment to other service users in the day care unit.

It was thought that a two-hour session was long enough to achieve our objectives for a session, but not too long for people who may be quite weak and frail because of their medical conditions. What we had not anticipated was just how much time might be needed after a session had finished. Sometimes members needed to stay behind to talk further before they were ready to return home. Also, the group leaders needed time to debrief; sometimes the emotional impact of the meetings was such as to need a long time to debrief (well over an hour).

It was noted above that the original plan was to set up the pilot study for six months initially. When sessions are not happening on a weekly basis, there is a lot to recap and also a lot will have happened to members in the intervening time. So whereas a group which meets on a weekly basis might run for 6 to 8 weeks, six sessions proved insufficient for the Quarry and Calder Groups. They both ran for a year. The Morrison Group has been running for 11 months at the time of writing and it is envisaged to run for another four months.

Open or closed groups?

The basic consideration for groupwork is whether the proposed group should be open or closed. An open group usually runs indefinitely and members can join or leave it when they want. A closed group has an accepted membership and runs for a set period of time. Hall and Lloyd succinctly outline both the advantages and disadvantages regarding open and closed groups, and these were given due consideration when preparing for the Beyond Existing groups (see Table 2.4 overleaf).

It was decided to run the Beyond Existing Groups as open groups, because it was thought that there might be further referrals as the project progressed. Sanderson sums up the advantages which we thought were pertinent to our work:

> Open groups are best suited to long term, unlimited group therapy which have more flexibility for group members to leave and return. The advantage of open groups is that the long-standing members can provide insight and examples of how they have coped with their difficulties and faced problems. (Sanderson 1995, p.197)

This was very true in the cases of Vera, Anna and Edna. In the Calder Group Vera and Anna were both very supportive to Marjorie. As the group was running Marjorie was diagnosed as having diabetes. Anna's husband had also been diabetic, so Anna was able to talk about the difficulties of being diagnosed and gave helpful suggestions about meals. Vera could empathise with Marjorie about the degree and effect of emotional abuse or 'mental cruelty' as they put it. Edna became a role model for most of the members of the Morrison Group after she told her story from start to finish about the rape she had experienced and indicated in following sessions how she

**Table 2.4 Open and closed groups:
advantages and disadvantages**

Open groups	
Advantages	*Disadvantages*
Access available when women want it.	New members may feel excluded from group culture.
New members can prevent group becoming stagnant.	New members may not know group information which is important to aid their understanding of another member's problems.
Members may find it easier to leave the group when they want.	Older members may not want to repeatedly share the same information with new members.
Reduces the 'secretive' nature of an incest survivors' group and may contribute to breaking silence about sexual abuse.	Possibly greater risk of breaches in confidentiality.
Repeated sharing of information lessens the power of the secret of sexual abuse.	Group may find it hard to resolve conflicts between group members with arrival of new members and uncertain attendance.
Members at different stages can give each other encouragement and support.	
Not dependent on 'viable' number of members. Allows women control over how they use the group in terms of attendance and input.	

Closed groups	
Advantages	*Disadvantages*
Members can get to know each other well over a period of time.	Women may find it hard to leave if group is not meeting their needs.
Group can move on together from one issue to the next.	Women may be discouraged if they have to wait to join.
Easier to plan group activities together.	A limited number of sessions may not be enough for some women to trust, feel safe.
Easier to establish and maintain group rituals and rules.	Women may not feel committed to the group because of its short time-scale.
Trust may be more easily established because no new members join.	More formalised structure may result in feelings of less control by members.

Note: 'Open and closed groups: advantages and disadvantages' from L. Hall and S. Lloyd's *Surviving Child Sexual Abuse* (1989) is reproduced by permission of the Falmer Press, London.

had healed through attending the group. This was particularly helpful and insightful to new members when they first attended the group.

Although Beyond Existing was being set up for older people who might have somewhat different needs from those of younger adults, attention was given to the literature which exists on incest groups and other survivor groups when discussing how the groups should be run. This was put together with the leaders' previous experiences of running other types of groups with older people.

Referrals

It is extremely difficult for most victims to admit to someone that they have been abused. In many cases victims have been threatened by the abuser, so much so that they are terrified of disclosing and fear the possible repercussions. Where abuse has occurred in childhood the abuser may have told the victim 'to keep it a secret' and in fact the child does this into later adulthood. There is also the fear that they will not be believed when they do disclose. This is particularly true for older people who were brought up to believe that if you had a problem you kept it to yourself, or had been told 'you've made your bed so lie in it'.

Consequently, many victims may have believed that this was happening only to them. Few victims who participated in focus groups said that they had known anyone else who had been a victim of child abuse or domestic violence (Pritchard 2000). Male victims have the added problem of usually being stereotyped as perpetrators of abuse rather than as the victims. So how did we get people to participate in the groups for survivors?

Publicity

It was important to publicise the groups and their purpose in the local area. The problem at the outset was that our funding was limited. Some was received from the Joseph Rowntree Foundation, and Churchtown Social Services agreed to give donations in kind to help with publicity, venues and refreshments.

Using the media

Local newspapers were approached and asked to run articles on the subject of elder abuse with a view to publicising the advent of the support groups. The response from the local papers was poor, and once the groups were established it was necessary to pay for a monthly advertisement in a local paper which was thought to be read by older people. The following advertisement appeared every month:

Beyond Existing

Support Groups for Older People Who Have Been Abused

Groups meet once a month in Churchtown

Next meeting: Friday 26 January 2001.

For further information ring
– in the strictest confidence –

Telephone Number: 0101 123456

or write to

Beyond Existing, P.O. Box X, Churchtown

In a society where education is now given a high priority, a problem which is often not recognised is that many older people cannot read or write, so that written information may not have the required impact. It was important, therefore, to find additional ways of publicising the groups; national and local radio stations were approached. I spoke on a number of local radio stations and each time there were telephone calls into the station after I had finished my slot, requesting advice. I followed up each of these calls, most of which came from victims who were housebound.

Flyers/posters

Initially flyers were designed on A4 sheets of paper which could be photocopied easily onto attractive coloured paper to gain attention (see Appendices and below). These flyers were sent regularly to:

- fieldwork teams, home care services, residential and day care units within Churchtown Social Services Department

- other local social services departments on the borders of Churchtown

- doctors' surgeries

- local hospitals

- local churches.

The flyers were also blown up onto A3 sheets and displayed as posters. Flyers, posters and leaflets (see Appendices) were sent to the following people and organisations in Churchtown and surrounding county:

- Adult Protection co-ordinators (within neighbouring social services departments)

- Age Concern (local branches)

- Alzheimer's Disease Society

- Carers Association

- churches

- Citizens' Advice Bureau (Local branches)

- community psychiatric nurses

List continues on page 46.

Beyond Existing

Support Groups for Older People Who Have Been Abused

Many people, both men and women, are mistreated or harmed by someone during their lifetime.

It is very hard for people who have been harmed to talk about it because they might feel ashamed, embarrassed (especially if it is a family member who has done something awful) or they think that no-one is going to believe what has happened to them.

Adults can be mistreated or harmed physically, emotionally, or financially by family, friends or strangers.

It can help to talk about what has happened and this is the aim of the **Beyond Existing Support Groups** which are being set up for older people (men and women over 60). The groups will enable older people to:

- meet once a month
- talk in complete confidence about what has happened to them either earlier in their lives or more recently
- meet with other older people who have been mistreated or harmed
- have support from other older people who have had similar experiences
- obtain advice if required.

If you (or someone you know) are interested in attending a group please talk to:

[Contact details given]

Everything you say will remain confidential.

List continued from page 44.

- community safety officers, police
- domestic violence officers, police
- housing departments
- local authority residential homes/day centres
- libraries
- newspapers
- police stations
- post offices
- private residential and nursing homes
- radio stations
- sheltered housing complexes
- shops
- Victim Support (local branches)
- Voluntary Action
- voluntary organisations (who cannot be named because of keeping anonymity of local area) concerned with domestic violence and rape victims.

Articles

A positive response to the flyers was that I was asked to write articles about Beyond Existing in various newsletters and magazines. These included:

- a newsletter which was circulated to wardens in sheltered housing accommodation

- local community magazines

- church magazines.

A massive response was not expected, but even so the response was disappointing. Users of the day centres did respond by asking questions about the posters, and day centre staff did regularly talk about the groups before they started.

During this time, I continued to co-ordinate the Adult Abuse and Protection Project in Churchtown, which involved monitoring all the adult abuse cases. Monitoring forms were sent out monthly to all fieldwork teams, home care managers, and managers of residential and day care centres. Letters and memos were regularly sent out with flyers about Beyond Existing to remind staff about the groups. I also approached workers when I knew they had worked with someone who might fit the criteria for attending the groups. It became very evident that social workers were reluctant to ask victims if they wished to attend such a group. This will be discussed further in Chapter 9. At this time I also decided to follow up some of the interviewees from the original research project. I found that social workers had either closed cases or were not keeping regular contact with victims – even those who still had clearly identified needs. Seven victims from the original project attended the groups (3 women – Beatrice, Lilian and Vera; 4 men – Bert, Jim, Vernon and William).

Meeting the potential members – screening

Reference was made earlier to the importance of screening potential members. In some cases a social worker talked to the victim in the first instance, either alone or in conjunction with the group leader(s). Most victims were seen in a centre either because they had been admitted on an emergency placement or because they attended there for day care. The group leaders also made visits to private residential homes and to people in their own homes. Six people who were visited did not subsequently participate in the groups. It is important to acknowledge that groupwork is not a suitable way of working for all people; some people need one-to-one work with someone they trust. In some instances we found that groupwork can be effectively undertaken in tandem with individual work.

For some potential members, it was found to be important to meet with the group leader(s) before attending the groups. Beatrice and Lilian had been placed in private residential homes; they were visited and said they would like to attend. Vernon wanted to speak to both group leaders individually before making a decision whether to attend. Anna, Bert and Jim had the opportunity to find out about the groups while in the centres after emergency admissions. In these prior meetings the group leaders spoke about:

- the purpose of running the groups

- the leaders' experience of working with victims of abuse

- who else would be attending the groups

- safety issues

- confidentiality

- what would actually happen at the sessions.

The leaders knew many of the members before the groups started. Rachel had known some of them when they had been admitted to her centre as a place of safety. I had known some from their participation in the original research project. Even so, we thought it important to talk to each person individually so that they knew exactly what we had in mind about the purpose of the groups and what we hoped to achieve, and so that they could ask any questions or vent their anxieties. It was important to establish whether they thought they would get something valuable from attending a group. It was imperative that they knew that we would be focusing on abuse, and for us to know whether they would be prepared to talk about their own experiences/situations.

Referral form

A referral form was developed so that the leaders could have information about the victim on record (see below). When a professional or outside agency referred someone to the group they were asked to complete the form, having discussed this with the victim. If the victim met with the leaders in the first instance, the victim was asked to complete the form him/herself. It is important for group leaders to know whether someone has specific medical problems, dietary requirements, etc., and also to have an emergency contact number (e.g. for relative, friend, residential home) in case something untoward happens in the group.

In conclusion, this chapter has explained how the groups were set up in Stage 1, the practical and emotional matters which we, as leaders, tried to keep in mind, and what we learned as we went along. Similar issues and approaches guided our work in Stages 2 and 3. We were grateful to our members for teaching us the things which *really* matter.

BEYOND EXISTING
P.O. Box X,
Churchtown
Tel: 0101 123456

Application/referral form

NAME: .... D.O.B: ....

ADDRESS: ....

....

.... POSTCODE: ....

TEL. NO.: ....

EMERGENCY CONTACT NO.: ....

SOCIAL WORKER/OTHER PROFESSIONAL: ....

....

TEAM: .... TEL. NO.: ....

REQUIRES TRANSPORT: YES/NO

Does the applicant have any special requirements e.g. medication, special diet, mobility aids? Please specify:

....

....

....

Please give any other information you think might be helpful:..

....

PLEASE RETURN THIS FORM TO THE ADDRESS ABOVE

CHAPTER 3

Vignettes of Members

Before talking in depth about what happened in the groups, it may be helpful to the reader to present short vignettes of the members involved. This may help to make sense of what is to come in the following chapters. In total, 17 members were supported in the three groups; they had all been victims of either elder or adult abuse:

Table 3.1 Types of elder/adult abuse experienced		
Category of abuse	*Number of victims*	*% of total*
Financial	9	53
Physical	9	53
Emotional	8	47
Neglect	7	41
Sexual	7	41
Systemic	2	12

Table 3.2 The members				
Member	*Age**	*Type of elder/ adult abuse*	*Previous abuse*	*Abuser(s)*
Anna	82	EN		Care staff
Beatrice	93	F	CA	Carer/gangs/brother
Bert	68	FN		Son
Deborah	45	PES	DV	Husband
Edna	72	S		Boyfriend
Hilary	54	PEFN	DV	Friends/husband
Jim	76	PEFS	DV	Wife
Kathleen	56	PF	DV	Daughter/husband
Lilian	75	PEF	CA/DV	Son/partners/brother
Marjorie	55	PE		Husband
Polly	70	Systemic		Agencies
Sharon	39	S	CA	Stepfather/father
Susan	61	EFN	DV	Carers/son/husband
Vera	64	PEFNS	DV	Husband
Vernon	80	N	CA	Wife/father/housekeeper
Vicky	49	PS; Systemic	CA/DV	NHS/husband/foster mother
William	79	PFNS		Friend

* age when starting to attend the group

Elder/adult abuse: recent abuse experienced and/or reason for referral to the group

Abuser: relating to both recent and past abuse experienced

Key to types of elder abuse

P = physical   S = sexual

E = emotional   CA = child abuse

F = financial   DV = domestic violence

N = neglect

Table 3.2 gives a summary of the members' experiences of abuse in earlier and later life. Five members (29%) had been victims of child abuse; eight members (47%) had been victims of earlier domestic violence.

1. ANNA (Calder Group)

Background

Anna is an 82-year-old widow who lost her husband very recently. They had both moved into residential care because of ill-health. Anna has severe breathing problems and uses oxygen, but tried to be as active as possible. She is perfectly mentally sound, enjoys talking to people and has recently become interested in using a computer.

Elder/adult abuse

Anna was emotionally abused and neglected by the care staff in the residential home. The situation became so bad that her social worker arranged an emergency placement in a centre.

Previous abuse

None.

Expectations of the group

Anna was very reticent about attending the group because she said she received enough support and did 'enough talking', because she was seeing a counsellor at the hospice where her husband had died.

Areas worked on

- abuse experienced in the residential home
- alternative accommodation
- bereavement.

Outcomes

Anna remains in the same unit with regular respite care in the centre.

2. BEATRICE (Quarry Group)

Background

Beatrice is 93 years old and has been living in a private residential home for two years. She never married and has always worked. She has strong religious beliefs. She participated in the original research project.

Elder/adult abuse

Beatrice was a 'multiple victim' in the sense that she had been financially abused both by a carer and by local gangs of children.

Previous abuse

Beatrice had been sexually abused by her brother since the age of eight; she gave birth to a baby girl when she was 16 years old but the baby died when it was a few days old.

Expectations of the group

Beatrice was very willing to attend the group and mixed well with the other members. It became evident during group meetings that she did not want to talk about the sexual abuse she experienced as a child, but she willingly talked about the 'hard life' she had experienced, which did include neglect and emotional abuse. She also wanted to discuss some of the losses experienced in her life, but not the death of her daughter.

Area worked on

- life review.

Outcomes

Attending the group gave Beatrice the opportunity to meet up with old friends and care staff she had known in the centre, and she was also able to make new friends in the group. This was very important to her because she had always been and felt very lonely and isolated throughout her life. For Beatrice the group became a social event. By the time the group finished, a full life review had been completed.

3. BERT (Quarry Group)

Background

Bert was 68 years old and terminally ill with bowel and liver cancer. He had been admitted to a place of safety in a centre.

Elder/adult abuse

Bert had been financially abused and neglected by his son, and he had suffered gross physical neglect. He was living in a room behind his son's garage where there were no cooking or washing facilities.

Previous abuse

None.

Expectations of the group

Support.

Areas worked on

- action regarding the abuse related to police and solicitor
- preparation for death.

Outcomes

Bert died while the group was running.

4. DEBORAH (Morrison Group)

Background

Deborah is a 45-year-old woman with moderate learning dis-abilities; she also has epilepsy. She is married to Michael, who is said to be blind (one social worker has queried whether this is true). Michael has been known to mental health services; he has been diagnosed as having a personality disorder.

Elder/adult abuse

Deborah is a victim of domestic violence. Michael is physically and sexually violent towards her; she has had several admis-sions to hospital after being attacked. One admission was when she overdosed and she admitted this was a suicide attempt after being abused. Michael controls everything Deborah does and sometimes withholds medication. He often prevents her from attending hospital appointments, or people from visiting the house (professionals, family and friends).

Previous abuse

Domestic violence.

Expectations of the group

Deborah did not know what to expect from the group but said she wanted to come 'to get out of the house'.

Areas worked on

- opportunity to talk about the abuse

- assertiveness training

- developing hobbies (Deborah started doing embroidery).

Outcomes

Deborah is still living in an extremely violent situation, but there have been occasions when she has stood up for herself and refused to be dominated by Michael. She also managed to spend a fortnight on her own while Michael went away. She had thought she 'wouldn't survive'.

5. EDNA (Morrison Group)

Background

Edna is a 72-year-old widow who lives in another town. She came to Churchtown Cathedral because she wanted to ask the Provost for help. He could not see her but she found a Beyond Existing leaflet in the cathedral and contacted us.

Elder/adult abuse

Edna had been raped thirty-six years ago. Her partner had tried to force her into prostitution.

Previous abuse

As above.

Expectations of the group

Edna had never told anyone about the rape, but she often thought about it and felt the need to tell someone. She wanted to talk to the group about what had happened and 'to feel better'.

Areas worked on

Edna attended several sessions and then felt ready to tell her story. With the agreement of other members a whole session was given to Edna telling her story from start to finish.

Outcomes

Edna says she has healed completely. She now supports other members of the Morrison Group and is seen as a role model.

6. HILARY (Morrison Group)

Background

Hilary is a 54-year-old woman who is living in sheltered accommodation. She suffers with severe depression.

Elder/adult abuse

Hilary was physically, emotionally, financially abused and neglected by friends with whom she had gone to live, having lived at various addresses after leaving her husband. The friends were a woman and her son, who uses drugs.

Previous abuse

Hilary had been a victim of domestic violence. Her husband had an alcohol problem. She left him and her three children.

Expectations of the group

To be more reassured.

Areas worked on

- talking about the effects of alcohol
- effects of domestic violence
- building self-esteem
- assertiveness training.

Outcomes

Hilary continues to attend the Morrison Group, which she says is helping her. She still gets very depressed. She receives support from a social worker and a home care agency.

7. JIM (Quarry Group)

Background
Jim was 76 years old and had been a victim of domestic violence all through his married life.

Elder/adult abuse
Jim was physically, emotionally, financially and sexually abused by his wife.

Previous abuse
Physical and emotional abuse by wife.

Expectations of the group
Support in making decisions about the future.

Areas worked on

- building self-esteem
- looking at options for the future
- maintaining safety.

Outcomes
Jim's wife found out where he had moved to after an emergency placement; she started visiting when the group was meeting. Jim then died very suddenly.

8. KATHLEEN (Morrison Group)

Background
Kathleen is 56 years old and has been diagnosed as schizophrenic. She has a speech impediment which makes it quite hard to understand her at first. She was living with her daughter who was known to mental health services.

Elder/adult abuse
Kathleen was physically and financially abused by her daughter, of whom she was terrified.

Previous abuse
Domestic violence from husband.

Expectations of the group
Kathleen expected people to tell her what to do as she could not make decisions for herself. She also thought people would do things for her; she asked leaders to make phone calls, write letters, etc.

Areas worked on

- offering options regarding getting out of the abusive situation, i.e. accommodation

- legal advice.

Outcomes
Kathleen was sectioned and remains in hospital at the time of writing.

9. LILIAN (Quarry Group)

Background
Lilian is 75 years old and has been living in a private residential home for two years. She had taken part in the original research project. Lilian has experienced abuse throughout her life, but no long-term work had been undertaken to address either this or her alcohol problem.

Elder/adult abuse
Physical, emotional and financial by son.

Previous abuse
Lilian had been sexually abused by her brother when she was 14 years old. Throughout her adult life she was physically abused by her four partners.

Expectations of the group
Lilian wanted to get out of the residential home, and she also wanted attention for herself.

Area worked on
Sexual abuse by her brother. She did not want to discuss the abuse by her son; she seemed to accept that this was resolved and was not upset that she had lost contact with all of her children.

Outcomes
In the first few sessions Lilian refused to speak in the meetings at all, but she was adamant that she still wanted to attend. Gradually she did participate and was able to disclose to the leaders what had happened to her in childhood. By the time the group ended Lilian had worked through the feelings she had towards her brother and other family members. One block which remained was that Lilian denied that she had had 17 children. She only talked about the 6 who were still alive.

Lilian always felt safe with Beatrice, but also started to trust Vernon and William. In some meetings she took the lead and told other members what she thought they should do with their lives. By the end of the group Lilian felt easier in the company of men generally, and less fearful.

10. MARJORIE (Calder Group)

Background

Marjorie is 55 years old and had been the sole carer for her second husband, who had suffered severe strokes. She suffered from depression and high blood pressure; while the group was running she was diagnosed as being diabetic.

Elder/adult abuse

Physical and emotionally abused by her husband.

Previous abuse

None.

Expectations of the group

Marjorie was referred to the group by her social worker. Marjorie herself was unsure about how the group could help her and was frightened because she said she was 'not good talking to people but would give it a try'. It gave her an opportunity to get out of the house.

Areas worked on

- current abuse being experienced
- her feelings
- whether to leave the abusive situation/give up the caring role.

Outcomes

Marjorie made the decision to put her husband in permanent residential care; she could no longer manage because of her own ill-health. Her husband died shortly after being placed. Marjorie became angry with the social worker and the group.

11. POLLY (Quarry and Calder Groups)

Background

Polly is 70 years old and was the sister of Bert. She was very angry after Bert died and asked Bert's social worker if she could come to the group he had attended because she wanted to meet the people who had supported him. Polly is very active in her local community and supports older people by running luncheon clubs, organising trips, etc.

Elder/adult abuse

Polly felt 'the system' (police and the 'so-called welfare state') abused her because it had let her brother down.

Previous abuse

None.

Expectations of the group

Polly wanted to meet with the group members and leaders in the Quarry Group who had supported her brother. She later transferred to the Calder Group which was located nearer to where she lived. There were ongoing issues regarding Bert's will and financial abuse. She wanted advice and support regarding these matters.

Areas worked on

- anger towards the people who had let her brother down
- probate.

Outcomes

- Polly could vent her anger and gained practical advice on how to proceed with matters which were outstanding
- bereavement and reminiscence work.

12. SHARON (Morrison Group)

Background

Sharon, aged 39 years, was referred to the group by her community psychiatric nurse. She has a long-standing history of depression and suicide attempts stemming from sexual abuse experienced from her father and stepfather.

Elder/adult abuse

Sexual abuse from Sharon's stepfather continued into adulthood. Her three daughters were fathered by her stepfather; she has one son.

Previous abuse

Child sexual abuse from father and then stepfather.

Expectations of the group

Sharon was very frightened when she attended the first session; she said she did not know what it would be like.

Areas worked on

- past abuse
- problems with son
- problems with youngest daughter who is in foster care.

Outcomes

Sharon continues to have good and bad times. Her attendance at the group is erratic; she uses it when she is going through a down phase. She comes to see Edna 'because she makes me laugh. I wish I could be like her.' When she is not attending, the leaders maintain contact with Sharon by phone and letter.

13. SUSAN (Morrison Group)

Background
Susan is 61 years old and was living in residential care when she was referred to the group. She is a recovering alcoholic. She has recently moved into another residential home.

Elder/adult abuse
Susan was financially abused by her son, who placed her in a residential home and sold all her belongings without her knowledge. Whilst she was in the home, she was financially abused by one of the care assistants. At the time of writing the police are investigating this. She was also emotionally abused and neglected by staff.

Previous abuse
Victim of domestic violence.

Expectations of the group
Susan did not want to attend the group initially, but her social worker persuaded her to give it a try.

Areas worked on
- financial abuse
- problems within the residential home
- empowerment and assertiveness – care staff were not allowing Susan to go out of the home
- regenerating interest in hobbies and leisure pursuits
- literacy.

Outcomes
Susan has taken many positive steps since participating in the group. She has chosen to move to another residential home, where she has blossomed. She has started taking an interest in

her own appearance and doing things she used to do – sewing, baking.

14. VERA (Calder Group)

Background

Vera is 64 years old and currently lives in a bungalow with one of her sons, who has learning disabilities. Her health is not good and she has been undergoing extensive tests during the past year. Vera participated in the original research project.

Elder/adult abuse

Physical, emotional, financial, sexual abuse and neglect by her husband.

Previous abuse

Victim of domestic violence throughout her marriage.

Expectations of the group

- wanted to talk to other women who had been victims of domestic violence.
- wanted to learn about why abuse happens.

Areas worked on

- explanations concerning abuse and violence
- hopes for the future – setting objectives.

Outcomes

Vera's attendance at the group was erratic. The positive outcome was that she wrote extensively in her journal about her experiences and her feelings, and she also wrote poetry (some of which is reproduced in Chapter 8).

15. VERNON (Quarry Group)

Background
Vernon is 80 years old and lives with his wife. He is extremely unhappy with his current situation.

Elder/adult abuse
Neglect, both physical and emotional, by his wife.

Previous abuse
Vernon had been emotionally abused and neglected by his father and housekeeper after his mother died.

Expectations of the group

• to be able to talk about how he felt

• to come to a decision about whether to move into residential care.

Areas worked on

• alternative accommodation

• life review.

Outcomes
Vernon kept making the decision to leave his wife, but then changed his mind. As the group finished, he and his wife had made a joint application to move into sheltered accommodation. Vernon had become extremely depressed and had started to show signs of slight confusion.

16. VICKY (Morrison Group)

Background
Vicky is a 49-year-old woman who is living with her 16-year-old daughter.

Elder/adult abuse

Vicky had been physically and sexually abused by her husband. She also felt that the 'system' was abusing her as she had been denied access to psychiatric services. She had attended one counselling group but had been asked to leave.

Previous abuse

Child sexual abuse by foster mother.

Expectations of the group

Emotional support and practical advice.

Areas worked on

- working through childhood experiences
- problems presented by daughter.

Outcomes

Vicky had to go into hospital for an operation. She missed some sessions and felt she did not have the courage to start again in the group, which had new members. It has been left open that she can rejoin whenever she feels ready. Dates of sessions are sent to her each month.

17. WILLIAM (Quarry Group)

Background

William is 79 years old and is living in a residential home, which he hates. People think he has some form of dementia, but this is questionable. He is confused at times and is obsessional about certain 'life events'; at other times he can be very rational.

Elder/adult abuse

William was physically, sexually, financially abused and grossly neglected by a friend who became a carer for William and his wife. The friend was also his wife's long-term lover.

Previous abuse

None.

Expectations of the group

William came to the first meeting not knowing what to expect, but said that he did want to attend when he knew what the group was about. He wanted someone to help him sort out his finances and to get rehoused.

Areas worked on

- current problems with residential home
- finances
- his wife's death.

Outcomes

Concerns about the home were reported and investigated. William would not accept his financial situation; he resented not having his pension and having to be in the home. The social worker would not undertake a new assessment. It has been agreed that William can attend another group in the future.

These, then, are the group members. In summary, the groups were as follows:

Calder: Anna (82), Marjorie (55), Polly (70), Vera (64).

Quarry: Beatrice (93), Bert (68), Jim (76), Lilian (75), Polly (70), Vernon (80), William (79).

Morrison: Deborah (45), Edna (72), Hilary (54), Kathleen (56), Sharon (39), Susan (61), Vicky (49).

The age ranges, particularly in the Morrison Group, seem wide, but were found not to impede the joint achievements of the members.

CHAPTER 4

Running the Groups 1
Practical Matters

One may think that if a person is experienced in running groups, then the work will be easy; this is definitely not true. There are the emotional aspects of running groups which will be considered later, but practical matters take up an enormous amount of time and will be the subject of this chapter. Potential leaders of groups should never underestimate the amount of time this takes up – before, during and after the sessions.

Before the session

Below it will be stated that there needs to be commitment from members to attend regularly. Each member was given a list of dates which were booked six months in advance. The list of dates was also given to other people who might be working with a member; for example, social workers, residential staff, carers. Problems arose when running the Quarry and Calder Groups, so that when the Morrison Group was set up reminder letters were sent out a week before each session.

Preparation for the leaders

It is important that the leaders of any group are well prepared before each session. This involves setting time aside to prepare, while acknowledging that you never know what is going to happen at the session; and sometimes the planned agenda can suddenly take a very different turn. As the groups developed it became clear what needed to be worked on; but sometimes, between sessions, things had happened to members of the group and they wanted to spend time discussing the event or issue. It was important to let this happen, even when it meant putting off some work until next time. There was a semi-structured format to each session which had been agreed when the groups were set up:

Table 4.1 Agenda
• welcome/refreshments
• short review from each member about what had happened in the last month
• agreed agenda items from previous session
• discussion about what to work on next time
• winding down

Before each session the leaders needed to consider:

- *Who is going to lead each part of the session*
  Each leader will have strengths and weaknesses. The weaknesses need to be worked on and sometimes it may be necessary to lead part of a session in order to develop skills and confidence. There may be tasks or situations which a leader who is learning groupwork skills cannot face at a particular time. Sometimes, it is just simply down to the fact that someone is having an 'off day'.

- *Whether there are specific responsibilities / tasks which can be divided up*
  There may be practical tasks which can be easily divided up to save time – e.g., before the session starts one leader organises the drinks, the other helps members who need to use the bathroom.

- *Whether members relate better to one particular leader*
  In the Quarry Group Lilian always wanted Rachel to toilet her and to take her into the dining room for lunch. Only on occasions would she ask me to walk with her. This was probably due to the fact that Rachel transported Lilian to and from the group and Lilian trusted her implicitly.

The room

The room should be prepared before the session starts. It is very likely that furniture will need to be moved and chairs should be set out in a way that is going to help the members feel comfortable (for example, in a circle which allows for adequate space between the chairs). Some members may require a table near them or other equipment (for example, Vernon needed to sit with one leg raised on a footstool). If the leaders are going to use equipment, this needs to be set up and checked. For example, a flipchart stand needs to be in a position where everyone can see it (taking into consideration that some members may have partial loss of sight); leaders need to know how to work the television and video.

It is essential that privacy be maintained throughout the session and there should be no interruptions or intrusions (for a summary on advice see box entitled 'Good practice tips'). This was not a problem for the Calder Group. The room used was located upstairs in a very quiet part of the building and staff re-membered that they should not intrude at any time. For the Quarry Group it was a problem. One of the three lounges on the ground floor in the centre was used; the door had glass in it. The problem was not with other service users entering the lounge, but rather with staff who would come in to speak either to a member of the group they recognised or to one of the leaders or when they had left something in the room. Even though staff were reminded before each session that there should be no interruptions, it still did happen. Eventually the glass part of the door was covered up and a notice put on the outside of it. This did resolve the problem, which did not recur when the Morrison Group was set up in the same location.

When rooms are given free of charge, sometimes it is diffi-cult to obtain perfect conditions. However, if there are going to be real difficulties, then the offer of a free room should be declined and another venue sought. Victims of abuse may be nervous enough about coming to the group; they should not have to be worrying about who might see them and therefore know why they are coming into the building. Any staff working in the building should be briefed regarding the confi-dential nature of the work being undertaken.

Good practice tips

- Remind staff and service users the room is in use.
- If there is a glass door, put sugar paper on the outside so that people cannot see in.
- Put a notice on the door:
  'ROOM IN USE – DO NOT DISTURB'

Transport

If leaders are going to transport some members to the group, they need to realise that very often, because delays occur, there is little time to 'psych' yourself up for the session. It is necessary to weigh up the advantages and disadvantages to the members. For some members it is very important to be brought to the group by someone they know and trust; and this may be one of the leaders. Initially Rachel thought that she had plenty of time to collect Beatrice and Lilian from their respective residential homes and still give herself enough time to get herself psychologically prepared. However, the reality was that Beatrice and Lilian were never ready when Rachel arrived, even though each home had been telephoned the day before as a reminder that the women would be collected. There was virtually no time for Rachel to prepare herself. She had the added problem of Lilian and her difficult behaviour.

If one leader is transporting members to the group, the other leader has to take responsibility for preparing the room (as already described) and welcoming members as they arrive.

If taxis are going to be used, a reliable and friendly firm needs to be found. Several taxi drivers made it very clear that they did not like transporting older people, who took up too much time getting into the taxi, and there was added work dealing with Zimmer frames, wheelchairs, etc. After trial and error a really good firm was found, who built up a good rapport with the leaders and the members. They also arrived on time, which is important. Members can get anxious when waiting to come to a group; they may have started thinking about issues to be worked on in the groups. If a taxi is late or does not turn up, this does not help matters.

Checklist

- Book taxis in advance.
- Ring residential homes to remind them about the group and collection of member.
- Prepare room.
- Check equipment for session.
- Make refreshments.

Ground rules

Ground rules for the groups were discussed in the first session and the following were agreed. The Quarry and Calder Groups adopted the ground rules set out below:

Ground rules (Quarry and Calder Groups)

1. Everyone will try to attend the group as regularly as possible.

2. Everything which is talked about in the group will remain confidential to the group. Nothing will be shared outside the group without permission.

3. No-one will be forced to speak or do anything they do not want to do.

4. There will only be one person speaking at a time. Everyone will have their chance to speak if they want to do so.

The Morrison Group amended their ground rules several times and the final version follows:

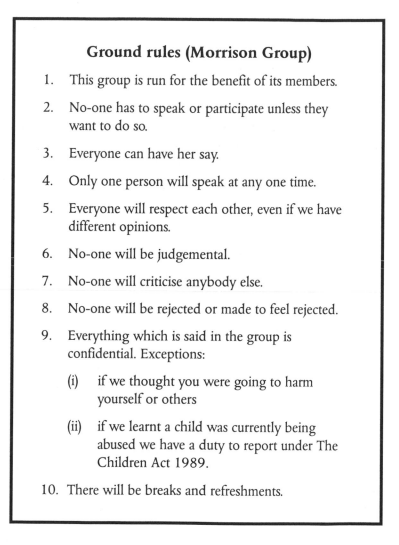

Ground rules (Morrison Group)

1. This group is run for the benefit of its members.

2. No-one has to speak or participate unless they want to do so.

3. Everyone can have her say.

4. Only one person will speak at any one time.

5. Everyone will respect each other, even if we have different opinions.

6. No-one will be judgemental.

7. No-one will criticise anybody else.

8. No-one will be rejected or made to feel rejected.

9. Everything which is said in the group is confidential. Exceptions:

    (i)   if we thought you were going to harm yourself or others

    (ii) if we learnt a child was currently being abused we have a duty to report under The Children Act 1989.

10. There will be breaks and refreshments.

Attendance

Commitment to attending a group is vital to sustain the activity and support. This proved to be a problem in the Calder Group. Marjorie and Vera both suffered ill-health and also faced crises which had to be dealt with; this caused them to miss sessions. Sometimes the session had to be cancelled on the day or there was a one-to-one session with the leader. None of the situations could have been avoided; it was not a lack of commitment to the group and the work being undertaken. This does, however, highlight the fact that older people may encounter different types of problems which will affect their attendance at a group, e.g. ill-health of self or of a dependent person.

Confidentiality

My experience in working with people from different service user groups is that many of them do not really understand what the term 'confidentiality' means. It is my belief that workers in many settings do not spend enough time talking about the boundaries of confidentiality. What confidentiality means to a person in their personal life may be very different to what it means in a work role. Workers should ensure that the service user knows that total confidentiality can never be guaranteed completely. Any information given to a worker belongs to an agency, not to the worker personally.

Explaining confidentiality to members of a group is just as important. Some of the members had social workers working with them, others were in residential care. It had to be made clear that information would not be shared with these helpers unless the member gave permission. The exception would be if the leaders thought that a member might be at serious risk of harm. This happened in the case of Sharon, who suffered severe depression and had a history of suicide attempts. We made it very clear to Sharon that if we were concerned about her we would inform her community psychiatric nurse; she accepted this and said she felt that 'at least somebody cared'.

Another consideration is information-sharing with families. Some members were worried that things they talked about would be passed back to their families. Again, they were reassured that this would not be the case.

Participation

One normally assumes that if someone is voluntarily attending a group they intend to participate. Such an assumption cannot and should not be made when working with people who have been abused. It may be extremely difficult for them to talk about their experiences and feelings. They may come to the group feeling safe but once in the group setting find it impossible to disclose further. This happened to both Lilian and Hilary. They were both quiet for the first two meetings. Hilary was polite and would respond when spoken to, but Lilian refused to speak at all – even when asked if she wanted a drink. They both made it very clear that they did not want to participate in the group's agreed tasks. This was acceptable to the group as the ground rules indicated that no-one would be forced to do anything they did not want to do.

Hilary explained that she just wanted 'to listen and learn what the group was about'. She did participate in the sense that it was obvious to the leaders that she was hanging on every word which was spoken and nodded openly when she agreed with something that had been said. At the end of each session she was asked how she felt and she said she found it 'very interesting'. However, after just listening and watching for two sessions Hilary started talking about the abuse she had experienced from her husband and was able to say how she desperately wanted to make contact with her children.

We were very concerned about Lilian and the behaviour she presented. Lilian had been a victim of sexual abuse and did not like men to be near her. She did accept Vernon, who was in the group from the beginning. Both leaders had known Lilian prior to her attending the group. She had been glad to see us when we first went to see her to invite her to attend the group. It was agreed that Rachel would pick her up and bring her to the session. Throughout the year that the group ran, Rachel never knew how Lilian would be feeling when she arrived at the residential home. Sometimes Lilian would be glad to see her; at other times she would be extremely agitated.

During the first two sessions Lilian never said a word. She would be 'chatty' before the group started but would clam up as soon as the work began. The positive aspect of this was that it was clear to us that she was listening to everything being said. At some points she became visibly upset and distressed. We always asked her if she wanted to go out of the group to somewhere quiet; she always chose to remain in the room. After the sessions we talked to Lilian alone to make sure she was all right to return home, and after the second session we felt we had to suggest to her that maybe the group was not the right place for her. She became upset at this and said that she did want to attend.

Our other consideration was how her behaviour was affecting the other members; they found it frustrating that she was not participating. Vernon took the lead in trying to get her to join in; he said encouraging things to her: 'What's going on in your head? It helps to talk.'

It was important to give Lilian her space and not to force her to talk. As leaders it is always important to ensure that everyone has their chance to speak, but sometimes it has to be made clear that it should be left to the member to decide when they want to say something and not feel forced to do so. The leaders have to make a judgement about how members are feeling and, if this is not clear, then to ask the individual concerned in private away from the group.

When Lilian came back to the third session she started to engage verbally and by the time the Quarry Group entered its second phase Lilian would often take the lead.

Respect and listening

A common occurrence in the Quarry and Calder Groups was that once the members felt comfortable and safe with each other they often wanted to say something all at the same time. It was necessary for the leaders to take control, to ensure that everyone managed to have their say and that certain members did not dominate the discussion. Marjorie had said at the first session that she found it difficult to talk to people, but in fact it was very difficult in later sessions to stop her taking over the discussions and interrupting people. When this happens the leader must remind the group about the ground rules. William tended to do this in the Quarry Group and it was Lilian who took control and frequently told him to 'shut up; you'll get your turn'. Out of context this may sound very rude, but Lilian was able to say it in such a way that William knew what she said was done in a kind way, giving other people time and space to talk. William often mirrored her behaviour with other members of the group.

In the Morrison Group the members were more respectful in allowing each other the space to speak. Sharon perhaps was the one who occasionally dominated, but when Deborah joined the group and the group became aware of her learning disabilities, Sharon took on a new role. She was very calm and encouraged Deborah to take her time in speaking. Deborah could communicate reasonably well, but was very nervous to begin with. All the group members were extremely patient and supportive towards her. When she became repetitive, they left it to the leaders to move her along.

Recording

It is essential that written notes are kept of all the sessions so that accurate records can be made. This was important for several reasons:

- to keep records for the leaders
- to monitor progress
- for research purposes
- to monitor one case of continuing physical abuse.

During the sessions it was my responsibility to take notes. This was explained and agreed with members when the groups were set up. The reasons for note-taking were explained and confidentiality issues discussed.

As Beyond Existing was part of a research project, it was necessary to keep records which could be analysed. Keeping research diaries was the main method in the qualitative study. After each session my notes would be discussed with Rachel in our debriefing sessions and then would be written up in more detail, covering:

- what had been discussed in the session – work undertaken and agreed agenda for next session
- observation of each member
- work which needed to be undertaken in the future
- agreed action/follow-up (e.g. with social worker, other agency, etc.)
- costs (e.g. taxi fares, lunches, etc.).

Deborah was continuing to live with her husband, who was extremely violent towards her. Each time she came to the group she would show the leaders and members the injuries he had inflicted. Rachel and I discussed with Deborah and her social worker that we felt we should keep bodymaps of these injuries. We explained to Deborah why we felt this was necessary, that it was a way of recording what was happening to her. Deborah had no objections to our doing this and we believe she had the capacity to understand the implications of it.

Debriefing

As well as leaving enough time to prepare before the beginning of the session, leaders should ensure that they have enough time to debrief with each other after the session. They should discuss:

- how the session went
- what they observed happening
- action/work to be undertaken
- how they are feeling
- agreement on recording.

Each leader should have supervision in addition to the support from each other. Rachel had regular supervision with her line manager, whereas in my research role I had an outside consultant with whom I had regular supervision. The advisory group members were also there to support and offer advice if and when necessary.

When there is only one leader

It was stated in Chapter 1 that an objective of Beyond Existing was to test out different ways of working. One test was to have just one leader for the Calder Group, whereas the Quarry and Morrison Groups had two. In the light of what has been suggested above, the following points need to be noted:

- the leader cannot transport members as s/he has to be present to welcome members to the session

- the leader needs access to outside support/ supervision to prepare for the groups and to debrief.

CHAPTER 5

Running the Groups 2
The Sessions

Before the groups began the leaders had some general aims about what they hoped to achieve, but were clear that the members should also define the areas they wished to work on. From the previous research project victims had said that they wanted to talk about their experiences of abuse and to get practical advice and information (especially those who were still living in abusive situations), so these were the main objectives at the outset. Additionally, the leaders wanted to facilitate the healing process if the members were ready. It was acknowledged that some members might not be ready for this, but the leaders would assess each individual's needs and capacity as the groups developed. In this chapter I intend to look at the work which was undertaken within the sessions of all three groups.

First session

People coming together for the first time in any setting may feel nervous for a number of reasons – whether it is starting a new job, joining a reading group, going to a night school class. The nervousness may stem from uncertainty – what is it going to be like? No matter how confident a person may be in life generally, the adrenalin may still pump rapidly in a new situation. So how must it be for a victim of abuse who is going to attend a group for the first time? Sharon reflecting back, said, 'I was scared stiff.'

Talking about abuse is extremely difficult to begin with and victims may not feel like talking about it at certain times. So they may feel very pressured in coming to the group, knowing the expectation is that they are going to face the whole issue of abuse in the next couple of hours. This is why setting ground rules is so important; so that members know that they do not have to speak unless they want to do so.

The leaders must aim in the first session to make the members feel safe and comfortable. A relaxed atmosphere needs to prevail. Time needs to be spent helping the members to get to know each other and acknowledging that coming to a group for the first time is anxiety provoking. The first sessions for all three Beyond Existing groups had the following agenda:

First session

- welcome
- introductions
- purpose
- setting basic ground rules and developing further guidelines if necessary
- leaders talk about their work experience and commitment to working with victims of abuse
- members talk about themselves
- expectations of the group – what members want to get out of it
- setting aims of the group
- use of journal/notebook
- dates for group meetings.

During the first session, the main objectives were explained again to the members; these had previously been discussed with the individuals when they met with the leaders prior to the groups beginning. It was made clear that they could talk about any form of abuse experienced during their lifetime, not just the recent abuse. The members were asked to talk about what they wanted to gain from attending the group.

The sessions ran very differently for the three groups, because of the levels of functioning and capabilities of the members. The members of the Quarry Group were more dependent on the leaders because of their medical conditions and abilities to communicate. Vernon and Beatrice both had hearing problems; this slowed down communication within the group. Vernon sometimes missed what was said, as did Beatrice, even though she used a hearing aid (the problems regarding her hearing aid will be discussed in Chapter 9). Members had to be reminded frequently to speak clearly and loud enough, but also to look at Vernon and Beatrice when speaking. The leaders needed to constantly check out whether the members were hearing everything that was being said and to be proactive in inviting them to contribute to the discussion.

During the first session members of the Quarry Group said they wanted to:

- talk

- go on trips

- get out (i.e. away from home).

Because many of the members did not get out very much, they welcomed the chance to 'escape' to the group. Some people may say that this is not a good reason for attending a support group, but we felt that it was justified, especially as some members were still living in abusive situations. One of the key findings from the original research project was that the older people who were interviewed individually or in focus groups were often lonely and a major need was for company. Many victims are isolated in that, even though they may be surrounded physically by people, there is no-one they can talk to about very personal matters. As William said: 'You can talk in here. Nowhere else will they listen to you.' William was living in a residential unit, where he was considered to be 'difficult' and not liked by staff. The group was a way of giving people an opportunity to meet other people, whom they may come to trust and feel comfortable with. This validated their involvement in the group.

Members of the Calder Group were more capable physically and mentally; I could often sit back and let the members take the lead. They were very clear in the first session about what they wanted from the group:

- explanations about why abuse happens, i.e. they wanted to be told the theories regarding what causes someone to be abusive, 'to make some sense of it' (Vera)

- to talk about how to handle problems with family members, e.g. son who was financially abusing; son who is behaving like his father did

- a life/company/friends.

As has been explained previously, members of the Morrison Group were younger and most of them had mental health problems. This group was more fluid in the sense that some members came and went as they felt they needed the group, other members joined at different times during the first six months. Overall their expectations were:

- to hear what others have to say
- proper support
- not to be judged
- to feel better.

Dates of sessions

The dates of sessions were set in advance and members were given a list of dates. The Quarry and Calder Groups met at set times and always on Fridays. The days and times for the Morrison Group varied and sometimes had to be changed at short notice; this was mainly due to members not being able to attend.

Methods

Recent books (Doel and Sawdon 1999) and journal articles on groupwork have presented new ideas for undertaking groupwork, some of which are exciting and imaginative and aim to get away from the 'sitting in a circle' approach. Beyond Existing involved the traditional approach; the members enjoyed sitting together and talking. This is what they wanted to do and the leaders did not want to impose their ideas on how the groups should be run. What was explained in the first session was that suggestions would be made by the leaders but the members did not have to agree with them and could put forward their own ideas. It is important not to push people to do things for the sake of research! As will be discussed below, the Quarry Group did refuse to do some things, whereas the members of the Calder Group were more willing to try out new things. Members of the Morrison Group were very hesitant when the idea of trying an exercise was first introduced. After the session where they participated using their journals and writing on a flipchart, they wanted more exercises and really enjoyed this activity: 'I loved it' (Sharon).

The following methods were used:

- discussion – focusing on certain topics

- exercises

- writing.

Discussion

Discussion was important for all three groups. For the Quarry Group this was the main way of working. In each group every session began with a review of what had been happening in members' lives since the last meeting, and then the group would be focused on a particular subject, task or activity. Members would have agreed on a topic at the previous session or they would be asked on the day what they wanted to talk about. The Morrison Group members were more proactive in asking for 'special time' right at the beginning of the session (or sometimes even before it officially started). Sometimes two or three members had specific problems, so time was allocated so that everyone could have time to express their own problems. In some sessions the intended topic/activity had to be postponed to the next meeting. The leaders made it clear that they could talk about anything they wanted to, but in addition reminded them that the purpose of the group was to focus on abuse. As a result, a wide range of topics were covered, but they could be grouped into:

- life review

- reminiscence

- past abuse

- recent abuse

- current abuse

- new problems

- the future.

Subject areas covered could be divided into themes which will be discussed in full in the following two chapters:

- disclosure about elder abuse

- disclosure about adult abuse

- disclosure about domestic violence

- disclosure about abuse in residential settings

- early life – family, school, work

- previous relationships – unresolved feelings

- regrets

- losses/bereavement

- loneliness

- depression

- power and control

- building self-esteem

- assertiveness

- hobbies/interests

- illness

- information about medical conditions

- alcoholism

- fighting the system
- housing
- finances
- preparation for death
- working on the future.

Exercises

Exercises were used creatively in order to offer different ways of working through issues and problems. They worked well for the Calder and Morrison Groups but not for the Quarry Group, who preferred to engage in discussion rather than undertake exercises. Also the levels of capacity were an influence in what could be achieved and what was worthwhile to the members. The groups carried out exercises in the following ways:

1.   Members worked alone (or with the help of leader/social worker) on a set task and then shared it with the group.

2.   The group worked together. A question/idea was put to them and they were asked to verbalise their ideas using a flipchart.

3.   An exercise was set as 'homework' and presented at the next meeting.

The tasks which were set in the Calder Group formed some of the discussion topics in the Quarry Group, but had to be introduced differently. The exercises were undertaken in a variety of ways in the groups but, in summary, they covered the following subject areas/questions (not every subject was covered in each group):

- Ground rules – what would make you feel safe and relaxed?

- What do you want from this group?

- Personal hopes for the future – where do you see yourself in six months, one year, five years from now?

- Think of a time when you were able to change something in your life.

- Think of a difficult situation. How did you deal with it? What got you through?

- When did you feel safe/unsafe in childhood? (This is an excellent exercise for facilitating disclosure about child abuse.)

- When have you felt safe/unsafe in adulthood?

- Think of happy and sad times.

- Think of strong and weak times.

- How have you coped with a loss?

- How have you coped with a death/bereavement?

- When have you been frightened?

- What do you fear now?

- What is happiness?

- What do the following mean to you – victim; survivor?

- What are your strengths?

- What strengths do you see in other members of the group?

- What constraints do you have in your life?

- Discuss an object which means something to you.

- Write six episodes of a soap opera – each episode is about an important time in your life.

- What are you good at now?

- What would you like to be good at in the future?

- What makes you trust someone?

- How do you gain trust?

- When are you not assertive?

- Who can you be assertive with?

- Who are you not assertive with?

- Think of things you can do to be more assertive.

- Think of positive statements which can be made to help you be more assertive.

- Pick a situation in which you are going to work at being more assertive before the next session.

- What do you like about yourself?

- What would you like to change about yourself?

Two examples of exercises which worked well

Example 1

This exercise was done in all three groups. Members were asked to bring to the next session an object which was important or special to them because it had helped them at a difficult time or given them strength in a certain situation. The expectation was that the member would talk about the situation and how the object had helped them.

Many members brought photographs of family members or people who meant a lot to them now. Sharon referred to her current partner as 'my rock'. Edna brought two things initially but then continued to bring other things occasionally. Edna was very proud of having been a draughtswoman and wanted to show members some of the drawings she had produced. To her the drawings were validation that she was good at something. Her abuser had made her feel that she was 'incapable' and often repeated 'you are insane'. Vicky showed members the coloured plastic bracelet which a nun had given her when she was nine years old. She 'holds it and thinks about things' when she is going through difficult times. The bracelet reminds her that 'not all people are bad'.

Vera brought the poems she had written years ago. Some of these were about the abuse that she had experienced, others were about things she thought about. She read the poems to the group, which had a very powerful impact on everyone. She then talked about what her husband had done to her over the years but also explained when and where she wrote poetry and how it helped her. I believe this encouraged Marjorie to write in her journal over the following months.

Marjorie said she did not have anything and did not bring anything to the next session. Months later a session had just begun when Marjorie said she had brought 'something special'. Out of her handbag she produced a box which contained a pair of earrings which her first husband had given her for the last anniversary that they were together. Marjorie then talked about the good marriage she had had and how looking at the earrings would help her to remember 'good times' when she was actually feeling bad.

Example 2
The results of this exercise, which engaged the Morrison Group and consequently got them enthusiastic about doing further exercises, are shown below. They were asked to think for a few minutes in silence about the words 'victim' and 'survivor'. Then they were invited to share their thoughts. One of the leaders started to write the key words down but then members were invited to write on the flipchart themselves. Doing this exercise opened up discussion about what had happened to the members and also how it affected them in the long term. The discussion was taken further by a follow-on second exercise which encouraged members to talk about their strengths in dealing with abuse and what constraints it put on them. The key points from the flipcharts were typed up after the session and photocopied to give to members for the next session. When work was written up it was referred back to in future sessions and shown to new members (with the permission of members who had undertaken the work).

Summary of work from exercises undertaken with the Morrison Group

What the word 'VICTIM' means to you

- abuse – ongoing
- lose all self-esteem
- suffering – still
- pain in head
- physical pain
- emotional pain
- spiritual suffering
- screwing your mind
- happy-go-lucky
- worthless
- dirty
- vulnerable
- migraine
- nerves in teeth
- sad
- ugly
- sense of humour
- sensitivity
- empathy.

What the word 'SURVIVOR' means to you

- I don't know I will survive this
- be happy again
- what's that?
- still here
- resilient
- strength

- talk
- honest
- open
- trusting
- see things for what they really are
- protective
- goods.

Strengths

- artistic
- determined
- doing what I want to do
- enjoy it
- being retired
- compassion
- caring
- being able to share with others
- happy
- intelligent
- nice to get on with
- honest
- confronting the pain
- attractive
- role model
- mother figure
- defend children
- sweet.

Constraints

- head
- memory.

Writing

> By going back and writing about what happened, you also re-experience feelings and are able to grieve. You excavate the sites in which you've buried memory and pain, dread and fury. You relive your history. (Bass and Davis 1988, p.27)

During the first session, it was explained to members that some victims find writing therapeutic. It is a way of telling their story; the story could be kept private or it could be shared if they felt OK. Every member was given a journal; it was made very clear that if members did not want to use it they need not do so. It was explained the journal could be used to:

- write about a previous experience (abuse, loss, etc.)
- write about feelings
- write about events, thoughts or ideas which have occurred between sessions
- keep a diary
- undertake exercises.

Some members read from their journals to the rest of the group; Sharon asked me to read out loud from her journal which she used in a diary format to record her feelings and thoughts. Members were also given a small notebook which they could use for notes or reminders.

We got very different reactions to the idea of writing; some we expected, some we did not. I was aware that Vera wrote poetry and expected her to enjoy the opportunity to write expressively, which she did. I also expected Lilian to use this way of communicating because during the adult abuse investigation and during her interviews for the original research project, she would only 'talk' about the abuse by using a pen and paper. I had expected her to do the same in the group. I was wrong. She was adamant that she would not write at all. However, in later sessions when she started to engage with the group, sometimes she struggled with words. Her speech was slightly slurred due to a stroke. When she knew members were not understanding her, she would write the word down in the small notebook.

Privacy and safety issues were raised by Vernon and Marjorie. They said they were frightened that their partners would find the journal. Vernon said his wife was 'very nosey' and would read through it all. Consequently, he never used the journal. Marjorie's husband was severely disabled and if she put the journal away, there is no way that he could have got to it. With hindsight, this was the excuse she used not to write; Marjorie lacked confidence in herself, but also because of her depression she 'did not see the point'. Once again Marjorie surprised the group in a later session when she brought out her journal and said she wanted to read from it. Her writing was incredibly powerful; she could capture her emotions very clearly in words. She continued to write and shared the journal with her social worker, who was also very moved.

Some of the exercises which were used involved writing, and in the Quarry and Morrison Groups there were people who had literacy problems. Leaders must always consider that some older people may not be able to read and write; therefore, writing may not be a medium through which they can communicate. We talked to them individually about how to handle this. Once the groups were established and members trusted each other, some said they were willing to try the exercises if they could work with one of the leaders. In the Morrison Group, Deborah, Hilary and Susan were supported by their social workers and then by the leaders. Polly helped certain members in the Quarry Group, especially Beatrice, who considered herself to be 'a dunce'.

Self-esteem and assertiveness

The success of the groups was that everyone who attended became involved and told their stories. Not all of them felt healed. However, one area where it was felt that everyone made some progress was in building self-esteem and becoming more assertive. Many victims blame themselves for the abuse happening. Work was undertaken to explain it was not the victim's fault. In an ongoing group it is important to do some assertiveness training which can be developed and for which targets can be set. Below is a summary of the work which was achieved with the Morrison Group when they started working on becoming more assertive:

When are you not assertive?

- doing things to please other people
- if you don't want to argue
- when questioning your own intelligence/ability.

Reason for not being assertive: Not wanting to upset someone/fall out with them.

Who can you be assertive with?

- children
- people at work
- when it's for other people
- friends.

Who are you not assertive with?

- cousin
- when it is for yourself

- friends
- people in authority.

Strategies to be more assertive

- don't argue
- walk away
- speak your mind
- suggest things
- talk and explain
- repeat your wishes/choices
- remain calm
- positioning – hands on hip
- do it on your own territory
- raise voice a little (if you normally speak very quietly) to make yourself heard.

Positive statements which can be made?

- 'I want to…'
- 'I like…'
- 'It is imperative I go…'
- 'I *am* going.'
- 'I can get my hair done any time.'
- 'It's not good enough…'
- 'I'll speak to my social worker about it…'
- 'It is my right…'
- 'I'll get back to you on that.'

What do you like about yourself?

- friendly
- easy-going
- understanding
- caring (3)
- strong (4)
- staying power
- being able to produce something – an end product
- to do/make things
- willpower (2)
- honest
- sense of humour (2)
- appearance (3)
- skills – baking, knitting, sewing (2)
- being able to carry on (2)
- being able to carry through
- being able to read
- get on with other people
- patience
- don't give up
- good homemaker
- generous.

What would you like to change about yourself?
- being manipulated (3)
- easily influenced
- education: improve reading and writing
- improve mental arithmetic
- am easily talked into things
- not feeling good enough (for other people)
- the way I dress
- being more confident in talking

Some members were experiencing particular difficulties when the assertiveness sessions were taking place. Below are three examples of situations which were addressed:

Objectives for next session

Susan

To be more assertive with care staff in residential home. Work on refusing to be forced into doing activities. Refuse to spend time with other service user who has a drink problem. (This was important to Susan who was fighting hard to remain 'dry' herself.)

Hilary

To be more assertive with home carers when they walk into the flat without knocking, and use the master key.

Edna

To ask daughter for money she owes.

Between the sessions

As has already been acknowledged, one of the disadvantages of having monthly sessions is that there is a long time gap. An issue for the leaders was that very often members were deeply affected by the discussions which took place during the sessions. Time was allowed at the end of each session for members to talk about how they were feeling; and if there were concerns the leaders worked with individuals after the session had finished. From the outset members had a contact number so that if they wished to speak to a leader between the sessions they knew they could do so. All members commented that they thought about what had been discussed; it would have been unnatural just to shut down completely after discussing such emotive subjects.

It was important to follow up on people who were obviously deeply affected by the session. This was done by telephoning them during the same evening or the day after. Permission was also asked to alert people who might be having contact with them; for example, residential staff. The leaders were particularly concerned about Lilian when she disclosed memories and feelings about the sexual abuse inflicted by her brother. At this time, the leaders decided to visit Lilian regularly in the residential home between sessions.

The leaders were also concerned when Edna had used a whole session to tell her story, which was a big ordeal for her. She was contacted that evening and the days that followed. In fact, there was no cause for concern because the 'telling' had healed her and she felt 'wonderful'.

The leaders had many concerns about Sharon, especially when she did not attend a session. Efforts were made to keep in touch with her by telephone and letter. This was often difficult as she frequently changed her mobile number and moved to different addresses. But Sharon said she felt that people did care about her, and appreciated the efforts made.

It has to be said that there were some negative effects for other members. Beatrice said she 'loved' coming to the sessions but sometimes she was 'sad' because she thought about 'missing my family and what I have lost'. Vicky said she 'felt dazed' after the sessions, 'but not bad enough to contact you'.

CHAPTER 6

Themes and Stories 1
The Abuse

In the previous chapter a list of subject areas covered in sessions was given. The purpose of this chapter and the next is to give more details about the recurring themes that emerged during the groups' discussions and the exercises in which they participated. This chapter will focus on the themes and stories regarding the abuse which members had experienced both in later life and in childhood and earlier adulthood. The following chapter will discuss what themes and stories were presented when working through the healing process.

Disclosure about elder abuse

All the victims who attended the Quarry and Calder Groups had been abused later in life. Polly's abuse did not in the strictest sense fit into the usual categories of abuse – she felt she was a victim of systemic abuse; it could also be argued that her needs were neglected. This will be discussed below. The research project had taken a definition of abuse (see Chapter 1) which included five categories; members had experienced the following types of abuse:

Table 6.1 Types of abuse experienced		
Financial	6	Beatrice, Bert, Jim, Lilian, Vera, William
Neglect	5	Anna, Bert, Vera, Vernon, William
Physical	5	Jim, Lilian, Marjorie, Vera, William
Emotional	5	Anna, Jim, Lilian, Marjorie, Vera
Sexual	3	Jim, Vera, William
Systemic	1	Polly

Financial

In the original research project it was found that financial abuse was the most common form of abuse experienced by older people; the same pattern was found in the Quarry and Calder Groups. Six members had been abused financially, but in very different ways.

Beatrice had lost considerable sums of money when a formal carer took money from her on a regular basis. At the same time she was terrorised by gangs of children in the area who also took money from her. At the time, Beatrice appeared slightly confused so it was difficult to get detailed accounts of when the early adult abuse investigations took place. It was evident at a later date that this confusion was due to the effects of the abuse, not to any intrinsic cognitive impairment.

Bert had been systematically abused by his son, who used to take his cashcard (without Bert knowing) and make with-drawals from his bank account. £3000 was taken in total. The son also fraudulently set up standing orders to pay the rent for Bert's grandson's flat. Just under £1000 had been paid out before Bert realised that amounts were disappearing from his account. Initially, the police had not taken the matter very seriously and said there was not enough evidence to warrant an investigation. Bert insisted on going to see a solicitor about taking civil action. Once the solicitor started acting on Bert's behalf, the police said that they would take a formal statement from Bert and investigate further. Sadly, Bert died before this happened. After Bert's death, Polly wanted to pursue the matter and 'get justice for Bert', but no-one would help her.

Lilian was also financially abused by relatives. Lilian's children would regularly steal from her. After one of her sons had been released from prison she accumulated large debts and the bailiffs came to her door. The same son stole her television and video. Another son both physically and financially abused her and was the reason for Lilian making the decision to leave her home. One day she gave a note to the home carers which asked them to 'get me out'. She was admitted to a place of safety the same day.

Jim and Vera were financially abused by their spouses. Jim had always been very generous to his wife; whenever he had spare money he would buy her gifts but she said they were 'never enough'; she 'always wanted more'. In recent years she became obsessed with spending money and taking money from Jim. She took control of the attendance allowance. Jim eventually opened a separate savings account to protect his money.

Vera had always been kept short of money by her husband and had struggled to feed herself and her sons. She believed she had been financially abused throughout her marriage because her husband controlled their finances.

William was financially abused by Edmund, who previously had been 'a friend' but became the carer for William and his wife, Ellen, who was blind. Edmund was also Ellen's lover. The couple were financially abused by Edmund over a number of years. He persuaded Ellen to sign cheques over to him, and he also got her signature so that he could make withdrawals from her joint accounts with William.

Neglect

Anna and her husband were emotionally abused and neglected in a residential home. This will be discussed in full below.

Emotional neglect has already been mentioned in considering emotional abuse (above). It was Vernon who talked most about neglect in the groups. He believed that he was both physically and emotionally neglected by his wife. He talked at length about being lonely and being left on his own while 'she goes out and enjoys herself'.

Bert, William and Vera were victims of gross physical neglect. Bert had been living in a room at the back of his son's garage; there were no washing or cooking facilities. The meals which his son provided did not suit his health requirements and he rarely had all the equipment for his stoma care. William also lived in squalid conditions. When he was admitted to care his skin was ingrained with dirt. When Vera had been ill, her husband had not fed her, so that over a seven-month period she became so malnourished she could not move from the settee. One of her sons eventually rang for an ambulance and it was thought on admission to hospital that she would die. Her body was covered in sores.

Physical

The victims who had been physically abused talked about extreme forms of physical violence. They had been kicked, slapped and punched. Vera in particular went into graphic detail about what her husband had done not only in recent years, but also throughout the marriage. Lilian had suffered physical and financial abuse from her various children. On one occasion she had had to crawl out of the front door for help; a passer-by had come to her rescue. Marjorie's husband had been violent towards herself and one of his sons: 'He picked on him till he left.'

Jim had a tracheotomy tube in his throat. When his wife was angry she would threaten to pull it out and she had done so on two occasions. Various professionals witnessed her violent outbursts. The last time Jim left her she had attacked the police officer who was escorting him from the home. Jim's wife had two children from a previous marriage, but they would not have anything to do with their mother because of her behaviour.

Emotional

It could be argued that all the members had been emotionally abused because they had all been threatened in some way. However, it was important to define abuse from the members' perspective. Four members who had been physically abused talked specifically about emotional abuse and gave examples of how the abuser had done this. Accounts included humiliation and ridicule; shouting, swearing and screaming; bullying. Anna had been abused by staff in her residential home; this will be discussed separately below.

Sexual

It is important to acknowledge that men as well as women can be victims of sexual abuse. William had been raped by his carer, Edmund; he was also regularly forced into sexual activities with Edmund and prostitutes. Jim was forced to have sexual intercourse with his wife; he said he did not want intercourse and had explained to his wife that it was too painful, having suffered with cancer. Vera said that she was regularly raped by her husband. In 1991 when she was living in another area, Lilian alleged that she had been the victim of an attempted rape. The social worker's response to that had been (and this was verified on her case file): 'She has been known to adopt ploys such as this so that she can apply for a day centre.'

Disclosure about adult abuse

In this section the recent adult abuse as disclosed by the Morrison Group will be presented. Members had experienced the following types of abuse:

Table 6.2 Types of abuse experienced		
Sexual	4	Deborah, Edna, Sharon, Vicky
Physical	4	Deborah, Hilary, Kathleen, Vicky
Financial	3	Hilary, Kathleen, Susan
Emotional	3	Deborah, Hilary, Susan
Neglect	2	Hilary, Susan
Systemic	1	Vicky

Sexual

Edna, Sharon and Vicky were quite insistent about defining the sexual abuse they experienced as rape. Deborah said 'he forces me to do it' but did not use the word 'rape'.

Edna had been raped 36 years ago by a man she was seeing. At the time she was a widow and bringing up two daughters. Edna referred briefly to the rape during several sessions and then said she was ready to tell the whole story. She could describe very vividly what had happened to her during the attack, in which she lost consciousness, and the injuries she sustained, which included fracturing the palate in the roof of her mouth. Her abuser had threatened her with what he would do if she told anyone and said, 'Nobody would believe you anyway.' He often told her, 'You are insane.' Edna said she never told anyone until recently because she was 'worried about what he would do to my daughters'. Another problem was that he was a well-respected member of the local community. Edna had told one of her daughters three years ago about it, but felt she needed to talk further about it and 'get it out'. Once she had told her story to the group, she was also able to tell her brother what had happened to her all those years ago.

Sharon did not go into detail about her sexual abuse; but she wanted to talk about the anger and other feelings she had about it all. This was the same for Vicky. At the time of writing both still needed more support and are nowhere near completing the healing process.

Physical

Deborah, Hilary and Kathleen had all been physically abused. Deborah is regularly physically abused by her husband, Michael, and has had several admissions to hospital over the years. It is thought he has a personality disorder. At each session, Deborah would show members the new injuries which had been inflicted.

At the first session which Kathleen attended she disclosed the physical abuse inflicted by her daughter, Ailsa, of whom she was terrified. She had been attacked on the morning of the session and was very distressed. Most of the session was given over to letting her talk about the abuse and what she wanted to do. Kathleen wanted her social worker informed, as she decided she wanted to contact the police and go to a place of safety. Kathleen spent the whole of the afternoon with her social worker and her supervisor. Eventually, Kathleen changed her mind again and returned home. The physical abuse continued over the next few months, during which time Kathleen's mental health deteriorated. After wandering the streets she was arrested by the police under Section 136 of the Mental Health Act 1983 and then later was detained in hospital.

Hilary had been physically abused by her friend's son, James, who had a drug problem. The police had been called to the house, where Hilary was found to be huddled in a ball behind the door of a locked bedroom.

Financial

Hilary and Kathleen were also financially abused. Hilary had moved to live with a new friend and her son, James, who took out credit and rental agreements in Hilary's name without her knowledge. Kathleen was financially abused by Ailsa, who had many problems herself. Ailsa had been raped three years ago and had a drug problem. She had spent all the substantial amount of criminal compensation she had received and then started physically and financially abusing her mother.

Susan's alcohol problems had developed as a result of the domestic violence she experienced from her husband; the problem worsened over the years. Susan talks about her son, Geoff, 'putting me in a home' and 'selling everything I had'. 'It was hard for Susan when members were asked to bring an object which meant something important to them, because she said 'I have nothing left'; all her possessions had been taken and sold. She also alleged that Geoff had closed her building society account without permission and had taken the money (£3000+). On her admission to residential care, Geoff kept Susan's pension book, cashed the pension, but never paid her any money. Susan became a multiple victim of abuse, because whilst she was in the home she was financially abused by a care assistant. Both matters are still being investigated by the police.

Emotional

The abuses described above which Hilary and Susan experienced included emotional abuse – verbal, intimidation, ridicule. These forms of emotional abuse were also experienced by Deborah. Michael was always telling her she was incapable of doing things and saying that 'the house is filthy', which really hurt Deborah as she enjoys doing housework and believes this is one thing she can do well. She gave many examples of things Michael said to her but the most common ones were: 'You're a liar'; 'You're a bastard.' On one occasion he had been calling her these names as he pushed her into a pile of nettles; the sting marks were still evident when she attended the session.

Neglect

Clearly Susan's emotional needs were also neglected. She was placed in a residential home which had high dependency levels; the majority of the residents did not have full mental capacity. Therefore, there was no-one she could communicate with, except the staff, who told her that she was 'not allowed out'. Susan was very depressed because of the abuse she had previously experienced and the current neglect, because she was not receiving any stimulation at all. It was very evident from her behaviour in the group that she was certainly capable of interacting and physically doing useful things. When she moved to another home this was proven. Staff there were also over-protective towards her but at least she felt stimulated. She started going out and regained interest in previous hobbies, which she continued to develop by discussion in the group sessions.

Polly and Vicky felt that the social care and health agencies had neglected them, as will be discussed below under systemic abuse.

Disclosure about child abuse

Five members had been victims of child abuse – Beatrice, Lilian, Sharon, Vicky and Vernon. Beatrice did not wish to talk about the early sexual abuse she had experienced from her brother. She had told her story in full just once to me in private in the original research project. Her brother had started abusing her from when she was 8 years old; she became pregnant at 16 years, but had never told anyone about the baby she had given birth to: 'I had a baby when I was 16. It's true. I don't know how it happened. It lived, but there was nobody there to see it. It should have been in an incubator. It was a girl' (Pritchard 2000, p.66).

Beatrice had appeared to be slightly confused before becoming involved in the original research project; day care staff believed she was starting with dementia. After telling her story, the apparent confusion went away completely and her care workers were amazed at the sudden change in Beatrice. This is a classic case of how some victims just need to tell their story once. Beatrice knew that she could talk safely in the Quarry Group, as other members had also experienced sexual abuse, but she did not feel the need to do this. For her, once was enough. However, what she did talk about at most sessions was the emotional abuse she had earlier experienced from her father. She said, 'I was scared of him. I didn't like his swearing. He slapped me. He treated the boys differently.'

In the original research project Lilian had hinted that she had been sexually abused as a child but had not wanted to talk about it in detail. Through the work we were doing with the

Quarry Group, Rachel and I picked up a hint that Lilian now wanted to disclose but was finding it embarrassing; she would often become very agitated – wringing her hands, rubbing her legs. We therefore made it possible to talk to Lilian in private. We talked to her alone after sessions had finished, and Rachel also took her out of the large group and spent time with her; we went separately to visit her in the residential home in order to build up trust and also to check out that she was all right after the sessions (see Chapter 5).

During one session we both detected she was on the verge of talking about what had happened but could not get it out. She talked about 'being made to live with my grandmother. She loved me, they didn't'. She was telling us that she had been excluded from the family and felt that it was her fault. She eventually disclosed her situation to Rachel whilst she was being toileted. She made Rachel promise not to tell anyone, in-cluding me, because it was 'a secret'. She subsequently dis-closed the same information to me and made me promise not to tell Rachel. We felt we had to be honest and open with Lilian; we both sat down with her and talked openly about what she had told us individually. Like many victims, Lilian believed that the abuse was her fault and that 'it was dirty to talk about it'. She was frightened about how people would perceive her if she did disclose the matter in the group. We worked to help Lilian understand that it was her brother who was in the wrong and that we certainly did not think any less of her. Hearing other people's experiences of abuse gave Lilian the knowledge that it is all right to talk about abuse; it is not 'naughty' to do so.

The final session of the group was hard for Lilian. Rachel and I believed we had gone as far as we could with Lilian. She had blossomed in the group and was taking a lead in advising other members. However, she became upset when we were evaluating the work we had done with the group and wanted to talk about the sexual abuse again. Rachel worked with Lilian on her own; she still needed reassurance that it was all right to talk about abuse. Lilian's case is an example of how some victims need the one-to-one relationship to disclose details, but they also need groupwork to support them in gaining insight and understanding about what has happened to them.

Vernon also valued talking to Rachel and me privately. Like Lilian, he could say he had been abused in childhood but found it hard to talk about the details. Vernon hated his father and could talk about what he did once Vernon was an adult; but he found it difficult to explain what his father and the house-keeper had done to him in childhood. Vernon's mother had died when he was 11 years old; his father engaged a house-keeper (and her family) to move in. Vernon did not get on with them, especially the housekeeper's son, whom he described as being 'cocky'. Vernon disclosed that he had been emotionally abused and neglected. He frequently said in sessions, 'I would never treat my children the way he treated us.' The incident which had really upset Vernon occurred on his wedding day. His father attended the church service but did not stay for the reception. He also felt bitter about the fact that his father had 'never touched or picked up my children'. Vernon had gone into the army in order to escape the abuse he was experiencing.

Sharon had been sexually abused both by her natural father and then her stepfather; the sexual abuse carried on into adult-hood and resulted in her having three daughters. She also has a son from another relationship. Sharon could talk about the abuse and her anger very openly and honestly. At the time she joined the group, her community psychiatric nurse was sup-porting her in reporting the abuse to the police, who re-sponded to the allegations very slowly. Sharon spent many sessions talking about how she feels 'differently' towards her daughters compared to her son. She acknowledges that she has mixed feelings; one minute she talks about 'hating' the girls because they remind her of 'their father and what he did to me', but then she goes on to say, 'I love them to bits 'cos they're mine.'

Vicky spent a lot of time speaking about the abuse of trust. She had been sexually abused by her foster-mother. She did not feel able to give details about what had happened; she was not ready to tell the story in full. She did talk about the dreams she had and about how she felt when she knew that her foster-mother was dead. She had also started to trace her natural family.

Disclosure about previous domestic violence

Eight members had been victims of domestic violence earlier in their lives – Deborah, Hilary, Jim, Kathleen, Lilian, Susan, Vera and Vicky. Their stories involved accounts of extreme physical violence and also of 'mental cruelty', as it was described by some of the victims.

Jim was a classic example of the 'battered husband syndrome' as described by Suzanne Steinmetz (1978). The physical violence had gone on for years, but became more extreme in later years, as will be described below. Like many female victims of domestic violence, Jim had left on several occasions but had returned, only for the violence to begin again. Jim was able to talk about what his wife did to him and was not embarrassed about this.

Lilian had been married four times and in each marriage had been a victim of domestic violence. The long-term effects of these relationships was that she developed a dependence on alcohol, she became severely depressed and had attempted suicide on several occasions. She had received little help from the professionals who had been involved, when dealing with domestic violence and separation in the past. Files from another area included very negative and judgemental comments from professionals: 'She has an evil personality' (GP); 'She is only getting what she deserves as she has been a very bad mother' (probation officer); 'Very difficult lady with a vicious tongue' (social worker).

Vera had also been a victim of severe physical violence from her husband.

Hilary and Susan had much in common because they were both abused by husbands who had alcohol problems. They helped each other to disclose the physical violence they had experienced and were able to empathise with each other. They developed a special bond with each other and both women started to speak out more in the group, whereas they had both been very shy in early sessions.

Vicky did not want to talk about domestic violence at all; she just wanted the group to know it had happened. She felt her current problem was facing up to the much earlier child abuse by her foster-mother, and the current difficulties she was having in getting help from the psychiatric services.

Disclosure about abuse in a residential setting

Anna and her husband, Abraham, had been abused when living in Fulton House, a residential home. The couple had decided to move into residential care when they felt they could no longer cope in the community. Abraham was suffering with dementia and had various medical problems; Anna has chronic airways disease and uses oxygen frequently during the day.

Anna and Abraham had had a temporary stay in the home before deciding to become permanent residents. However, very soon after they entered the home, problems started to occur. Anna felt that staff were not caring for her husband properly.

He was having problems passing water and was in a great deal of pain. On one occasion he was found lying face down in the corridor; it was thought he wanted to die. Anna was devoted to her husband and became very upset when she thought staff were not giving the help and attention she needed. On several occasions Anna became distressed and shouted; staff told her that she would be 'sectioned if you carry on like that'. Anna and her daughter complained to the social worker about the way she and Abraham were being treated. When the social worker talked to the manager of the home she was very 'hostile' and said the couple were very demanding. Anna was described as being 'abusive' towards staff. She was assessed by a psychiatrist who reported she was suffering with acute anxiety and depression.

Abraham deteriorated; after an admission to hospital he was found to have cancer and entered the local hospice, where he died. Anna felt very bitter that the home never sent her a condolences card and no-one from the staff attended the funeral, which for most homes would be normal practice. Anna was distraught after the death of her husband. She grieved very openly, but this seemed to be a problem for the staff, who interpreted her as 'being difficult'. The situation for Anna became worse. Staff were verbally abusive to her and threatened her: 'If you're not careful they'll be coming to take you away.' The manager told Anna that she was 'causing staff to leave'. Anna believed this and became even more upset. The social worker arranged for Anna to have respite care in another unit to get her out of the situation. The social worker formed a firm opinion that staff had emotionally abused and neglected both Anna and Abraham.

Over the next few months Anna continued to receive respite care in the Calder Centre. The social worker spent a good deal of time with Anna, discussing various options, but she said that she wanted to continue to live in Fulton House. Anna at this time had regular counselling sessions at the hospice where Abraham had died.

Anna attended the Calder Group while she was in respite care. Both her social worker and the manager of the Calder Centre thought Anna would gain something from the group. She was very reticent but after I met with her, she decided to attend. She fitted in very well with the other women and was particularly supportive towards Marjorie. However, she felt that her 'situation' – that is, the abuse she had experienced – was very different from that suffered by the other women, who had experienced domestic violence: 'Listening to other people made me realise I was lucky to be as I am.'

Nevertheless Anna can certainly be defined as a victim of abuse in the home after Abraham had died. There were numerous incidents when Anna was verbally abused (e.g. told she was the reason why staff went off sick), completely ignored (certain members of staff refused to talk to her), tormented by staff (e.g. they told her, despite knowing she was claustrophobic, that she could not have her bedroom door left open, and removed the doorstop); staff removed all the wooden coat-hangers from the wardrobe and sometimes refused help in changing her oxygen cylinder. She was adamant that she did not want to move to another home, but it was very obvious that the staff group did want her to leave, and made life very difficult for her. A formal complaint was lodged and adult abuse procedures instigated.

Systemic abuse

Systemic abuse is a term which is used more commonly in North America; it should not be confused with institutional abuse. By definition it means that the ways in which a system works constitute abuse in terms of the loss of dignity and rights. Both Polly and Vicky felt they were victims of this type of abuse.

Polly felt that her brother, Bert, had not been helped by the police with regard to the financial abuse he had experienced. When she tried to pursue this she was not helped by the police, the solicitor, the bank or the benefits agency. She felt she was blocked at every turn.

Vicky is an extremely intelligent woman who realised a long time ago that she needed professional help to deal with her problems regarding past abuse. She talked a great deal about problems accessing services, and also about the experience she had had in a counselling group where she had been asked to leave because she 'wanted too much attention'. She said that Beyond Existing was a totally different experience. Whilst attending the Morrison Group, she was still trying to access services and had lodged a complaint against a community psychiatric nurse.

Summary

This chapter has shown that members had experienced many forms of abuse. Everyone has an entitlement to be listened to in order to come to terms with themselves as well as others. Without doubt, *all* these people are victims; some are also (collusive) aggressors. The conceptual and psychological distinction between 'victim' and 'aggressor' is never clear – this applies in all walks of life, and is often apparent in the ambivalences of adolescence. Our job as helpers is to hear what people say, and to use this as the starting point of change (or healing). It is easy to start apportioning blame, but it is never useful or helpful to do so.

CHAPTER 7

Themes and Stories 2
The Healing

In order to feel healed, victims have to recall and, in some sense, to relive the abuse they have suffered, work through unresolved issues regarding it – notably their feelings about the aggressor and their feelings and evaluations of themselves as victims – and develop strategies to face the future, particularly when future situations may reactivate memories of humiliation, fear and incompetence, and thus reduce levels of social functioning. All these processes were addressed in the three groups, but the members also had other needs. For example, they needed to talk about other life experiences (not only the abusive situations) and issues they were currently concerned about. Consequently, a crucial part of the work was to undertake life review and reminiscence in broad rather than restricted terms. It was also important to provide practical advice and information, and to deal with practical problems as they arose. This will be the subject of this chapter.

Early life

Life review and reminiscence work became a major concern of the Quarry Group. This method of working enabled members to talk about their lives in general and at the same time facilitated the story-telling of abuse within a broader context of experience. Most members of the Quarry Group (with the exception of Lilian) had been born in the local area and had not moved away (except for time in the army). In the early sessions members were encouraged to talk about their lives and key events. Members reminisced about local places, activities, and people they had known. The three main areas members focused on were:

- family
- school
- work.

All had experienced very hard lives; many of them had lived in extreme poverty. Beatrice remembered spending a lot of time accompanying her mother to work. She herself had been put into service at a very early age and had spent the whole of her adult life 'servicing other people'. When choosing subjects to talk about Beatrice always said 'school'. In fact she had had a very hard time at school; she was bullied by other pupils who saw her as 'weak'. On one occasion she was attacked and almost blinded. This was clearly an unresolved issue for Beatrice and had affected her self-esteem throughout her life; it may in some way have contributed to the likelihood of subsequent abusive situations.

As the group evolved, members spent more time talking about their working lives. Lilian had had a variety of jobs, but enjoyed 'working the mills best'. Most of the men had worked down the pit. They talked about the work they did, incidents and workmates. Lilian joined in easily with this conversation because her father and brothers had also been miners; Lilian knew a lot about the work, the tools, and so on. Vernon and

William had known each other years ago, and talked about people they knew in common.

Previous relationships

Many of the members had feelings about people and situations, which they had never been able to express before. This was a crucial benefit that members gained from attending the groups. There were members who needed to talk about abusive relationships from the past, while others needed to talk about the feelings associated with how they had been treated. For example, Beatrice felt that she was the 'black sheep of the family'; she had been treated differently to the others. Others needed to talk about the good times and the successful relationships. For example, Marjorie often referred to her first marriage, which had been very happy, but sadly she had been widowed.

Regrets

Members also wanted to talk about their regrets and what they should have done differently. Many made the same comment as victims in the previous research project; that is, they wished they had left the abusive situation earlier. Through the sessions, members started to realise that they had unacknowledged personal strengths; many had seen themselves as weak before attending the groups, and their regret was that they had not realised their strengths earlier and done something about their situations.

Losses/bereavement

Every member in all three groups had experienced bereavement. In the Quarry Group the deaths of loved ones came up incidentally in discussions when doing life review and reminiscence work, but later, when Bert started attending the group, a whole session was dedicated to 'death' and how to cope with it. (This will be discussed below.) The significant losses for group members were family members.

Vera had been pregnant ten times, but only two children survived:

> I used to make sure my boys were well fed and I was literally living on a diet of cornflakes and milk which ended up causing malnutrition... I went into labour on 9 October 1966 and I lost the baby. It was a girl. She was only 1lb 2oz. I have lost eight. I had a girl in January 1965. As you know I have two sons living but there was a miscarriage between those two. In 1960 I miscarried in the August because he made one promise to me and that was that he would knock me into the fireside and I would always be pregnant. So he made the threat and carried it out but he didn't realise my life was on the line all the time... I had four pregnancies from January 1965 until October 1966. (Pritchard 2000, p.50)

Lilian had experienced many types of losses in her life. Like Vera, many of her children had died. Lilian had given birth to seventeen children, and only six are still alive. Lilian continually refused to acknowledge the children who had died. She was adamant that she only had six children, and said, 'The girls are the most trouble. I don't like them.' One daughter has an extensive criminal record; on one occasion she was on remand in prison for attempted murder.

Lilian had also 'lost' her living children when they were taken into care by the social services. At the time, Lilian was not capable of looking after them because of mental health problems and heavy drinking – all long-term effects of the violence she had been experiencing.

Bert and Polly were brother and sister, but both had also been twins. Both their twins had died – Bert's at birth, and Polly's at the age of seven. After Bert died, Polly wanted to talk about Bert and attended the Quarry Group initially in order to meet the people who had supported him, but then transferred to the Calder Group, which was nearer to her home.

In every session Beatrice talked about her sister who had died of diphtheria at the age of nine. She had been the family's favourite: 'She had beautiful hair. I was the ugly duckling.' At the beginning of many sessions, when we asked members how they had been during the past month, Beatrice often said she had been 'sad because I have been thinking about my family and what I have lost'.

Jim was one of thirteen children; all his siblings had died. Jim remembered distinctly the day he heard that his brother had died. He described vividly how he 'was blown to bits' in the Second World War.

Two years previously William's wife had died of pneumonia after she had been admitted to hospital and he had been admitted to a place of safety. William had been very confused on admission and consequently does not remember her death or having attended her funeral. I spent a lot of time telling William and the group how she had died and what had happened to her. On one level he seemed to accept what I said, but in later sessions he went back to thinking that someone had stolen his wife's body. He would not believe that she was in the grave. In a later session we invited William's social worker to attend a meeting (with permission from William and the other members) to discuss her death (and to validate what I had explained) and to help with other things which were bothering William.

Some members had experienced other types of losses. Hilary had lost contact with her three children, whom she had left with her husband. She experienced considerable feelings of guilt about this, especially as her husband had sexually abused one of her daughters. (A current activity is to try to find her adult children. Hilary wants to talk particularly to the daughter who was sexually abused, but thinks she will be rejected.)

Susan feels very alone in the world; it seems to her that she lost not only all her possessions but all the most important people as well. She had had a good relationship with her daughter-in-law and she knows she has a grandson whom she has never met. So another current piece of work is to trace these lost relatives.

Similarly, Vicky lost contact with her natural family when she was taken into care. While attending the Morrison Group she managed to make contact with her brother, but the meeting was not successful and this contributed further to Vicky's emotional problems.

Loneliness

Loneliness affected all members in all the groups. Even those who were living in communal settings felt 'alone'; Susan's situation has already been mentioned. Anna was fairly isolated in her residential setting because of the staff's attitude towards her. Rarely could these members express their feelings to those who lived with them.

Marjorie felt trapped in her carer role. Even when she had some freedom she did not use it: 'I don't see anyone for days when Jock is on respite.' She said she had 'spent my whole life looking after people'. When she married Jock, she took on his four children in addition to her own three; she lived in a household with eight males. Jock had a stroke and became very disabled. Marjorie's whole life was centred on caring for him. She recognised this as a pattern which dominated her life; that is, she lived her life for other people rather than herself: 'I've never had a life.' So an objective in the work undertaken with Marjorie was to try to get her to refocus on herself and what she wanted out of life.

Vernon said his wife neglected him. She had a very good social life, which meant that he was often left on his own for long periods of time. He resented the fact that she travelled miles to play bingo. During the sessions he talked more about what his marriage had been like and gave vent to his resentment. He talked about the little things that should have mattered. For example, Vernon has always liked a cooked breakfast. His wife had always refused to cook any kind of breakfast for him when he came in from a night shift. Vernon said he saw himself as being independent because he did everything for himself: 'She never cared for me.' He was angry that his wife got attendance allowance when 'she goes out all the time. She doesn't look after me.' Vernon said that they had 'nothing in common'. When asked why he married her, he replied: 'At 19 you don't know what love is.' Getting married was another way of 'escaping' from his own family; he came straight out of the army and got married.

Depression

Depression had affected all members at some time. Marjorie was the member who talked quite openly about 'being depressed'. She told the Calder Group how much she cried and about her innermost feelings at these times. Her health deteriorated so much as Jock became more and more difficult that one day she collapsed (just before a session) and was admitted to hospital. She was diagnosed as having diabetes, and was also prescribed medication for the depression.

At certain times Rachel and I became concerned about Vernon, because he seemed very depressed. This was first noticed when the groups went out to Christmas dinner. Vernon is usually a happy-go-lucky sort of person; he remained very quiet and withdrawn on the day, but said he was 'fine'. This withdrawal presented itself on a more regular basis in the following six months. Day care staff said he seemed confused on occasions.

Sharon had been referred to the Morrison Group by the community psychiatric nurse. She had attempted suicide on numerous occasions and was on a cocktail of drugs when attending the group. She was under the care of a psychiatrist at the local hospital.

As noted earlier, Kathleen also suffered from severe depression and acute anxiety. Her condition worsened over the months she attended the group. This was probably due to the fact that the number of assaults by her daughter increased at this time and were more severe.

Power and control

Abuse is about power and control. This theme came out in many discussions when victims were talking about the abuse they had been subjected to. Fear of the abuser played a great part in how the abuser kept control of the victim.

Marjorie in particular felt that Jock was controlling her completely, even though he was severely disabled. She went on to talk about how he had controlled her even before he became ill. She described the way he demanded sex as a way of controlling her; he insisted on her being face-down. On one occasion she had fainted during intercourse and he had left her unconscious.

Vera was able to share with Marjorie some of her experiences of being controlled. Vera's husband had always said he would keep her pregnant so that she could not leave. Also he would not allow her to have any friends, so she was very isolated and could not seek help from anyone. Latterly he did not feed her properly so that she became malnourished and too weak to get out of the house.

Hobbies

One of the findings of the original research project was that workers undertaking assessments very rarely spent time identifying leisure pursuits and recreational needs. That is to say, the need for stimulation and to combat loneliness was not addressed. Consequently, time was taken in the groups to find out what members liked to do and what their interests were in the past and in the present.

Lilian loved reading crime fiction and watching films. Sometimes it is assumed older people like to watch old movies; but Lilian was besotted with the actor Steven Siegal and liked to watch contemporary films. She had also loved to dance in the old days and talked about the dance halls, where she had met her first husband. She had also liked to go swimming. Beatrice 'was not one for dancing' but she had been to the local pub now and again. It seems that Beatrice had not had much fun at all during her lifetime and all she wanted out of life was 'to have food and warmth'.

Vernon liked to be as active as possible and 'to use my brain' by reading newspapers, doing crosswords, playing dominoes and cards; all of which he did when he attended day care.

Polly was very active in her local community; she liked to help older people. She was involved in running luncheon clubs, and organising day trips out. She had had an unhappy marriage and spends a lot of time at home in her own room where she 'knits and makes things for charity'.

Much effort was devoted to Marjorie in order to get her interested in something, but she just kept saying 'I've never had a life' and could not think about what she would like to do. Vera, on the other hand, said, 'Although it scares me stiff I want to meet new people and make friends.' Both Vera and Marjorie said they found it hard to talk to people they did not know, but in fact they could talk without any hesitation. They just lacked confidence in themselves and gave the impression of long-lasting low self-esteem.

As noted earlier, several sessions were spent in the Morrison Group on exercises to highlight hobbies and interests which members had had in the past or would like to do in the future. The following list summarises what members set as targets for the future:

- art
- baking
- budgeting
- cake decorating
- cleaning
- copy writing
- cycling
- dancing
- flower arranging

- getting round places
- jigsaws
- looking after dogs
- looking after animals
- making rugs
- needlework
- reading
- running the home well
- tidying
- trying out new things
- skating
- writing.

Most members could think of things they liked doing, but it was sad that Deborah saw her hobbies as doing domestic chores which related totally to 'looking after my husband'.

Building self-esteem

Throughout running the Beyond Existing groups it was evident that members were at very different stages in 'facing' their abuse and feeling healed. They all had at some time suffered from very low self-esteem; some still considered themselves to be 'worthless'. Linked with this, they blamed themselves for the abuse they had experienced. Marjorie said: 'I blame myself. I hate myself for letting it happen.' The point about Marjorie was that it took time for her to trust people. So she always said she could not do something and then in her own time (and privately) she would do it. Her self-esteem was

extremely low; she believed she could not do anything con-
structive or useful.

Beatrice felt she was a disappointment to everyone – 'I've
never been a scholar. Bit of a dunce' – and referred to herself as
'the ugly duckling'. Jim also had a very low opinion of himself:
'I have always been a weakling.' He had attended an 'open'
school between the ages of 11 and 13 on grounds of ill-health.
He had wanted to go in the navy but was rejected because he
was partially deaf.

The most dramatic progress was made by Susan after she
had transferred from one residential home to another.
Everyone who was working with Susan helped to facilitate an
increase in her self-esteem – social worker, care staff and other
group members. Susan started to see that she did have a
purpose in life. She became more active, took an interest in her
appearance, went to the hairdresser's and bought new clothes.

Building self-esteem was in great part helped by learning
that abuse was not the fault of the victim and by undertaking
assertiveness training (see Chapter 5).

Physical illness

Many members had ongoing medical problems. Vera's
absences from the group were due to ill-health. She underwent
extensive investigations during the year her group was
running. She was able to talk about her 'worst fears'. She was
also coming to terms with the fact that she would need to use a
wheelchair in the future to get about. She found this hard to
accept because 'it feels like losing your dignity'. Vera needed a
lot of support at this time, because it seemed to take for ever to
get the wheelchair delivered. I liaised closely with Vera's social
worker at this time. Vera was dreading its arrival.

Information about medical conditions

It has already been said that one of the key findings in the original research project was that victims said they needed practical advice and support. This was evidenced again in the support groups. Marjorie faced a major hurdle when she was diagnosed as having diabetes. She was overweight and did not look forward to having to keep to a strict diet; though in the event she actually did incredibly well. Anna's husband had been diabetic and so she was able to offer Marjorie a lot of information about food, cooking, etc. The fact that this was coming from a fellow member who had also experienced 'failures' in life meant a great deal to Marjorie.

Fighting the system

Polly had initially come to the Quarry Group because she said she wanted to meet the people who had supported her brother, Bert. She felt that other people, like the police, had let Bert down. When she came to the group she talked about Bert as a person and what his life had been like. She also explained her version of the abuse by his son. As noted earlier, she later transferred to the Calder Group because it was nearer to her home. This group proved to be better for Polly because she got more support from the women who, as a whole, were more mentally capacitated. Thus, Polly was able to go into more detail about the problems she had regarding Bert's will, probate, the solicitor, benefits agency, and so on. Simple things, like people not returning her telephone calls, made her angry and 'they don't give me any answers'. Many months after Bert's death she still felt angry that issues were not being resolved and 'nobody seems to care'. At the last meeting Polly attended she said, 'I just haven't the energy any more. I'm exhausted with it all.'

Similarly, Vicky felt she was 'fighting' the Health Service for services she was entitled to. She talked in the group about what was happening and how her complaints were being blocked; like Polly, she was not receiving any response.

Housing

Being rehoused was a major issue for Vernon and William. Most of the work undertaken with Vernon was directed towards getting him to decide whether he wanted to leave his wife or not. He continually changed his mind about this; at one session he would be determined to leave, while at other sessions he would be ambivalent. A major issue was where he would go if he did leave. So various options had to be put before him. We liaised with Vernon's social worker, who arranged visits to different establishments, e.g. residential homes, sheltered housing complexes. Vernon needed to work out for himself that he was not ready for residential care, but sheltered accommodation might be a good option. Certain things made him waver: first, that he might be lonely in a bedsit; second, it might not be that easy to arrange to get out (he liked to go to the local working men's club and his daughter usually took him); third, his savings would be used up in paying for the accommodation. By the end of twelve months, other members of the group were getting quite frustrated with Vernon and got to the point where they were very direct, telling him firmly to leave his wife. By this point Rachel and I had concluded that Vernon would never make the decision to leave; he had been given every possible option and probably would continue to think about leaving but would never actually do it. The final piece of work which was done with Vernon was to invite his social worker to the group (with the permission of the other members) to discuss the work that everyone had been doing with Vernon, and for Vernon to be clear that every option had been offered to him. The message we had to convey was that mixed feelings and indecision are natural in some circumstances, however irritating they may be to other people.

William had never wanted to be placed in residential care; all he had ever wanted was to have a bungalow. His social worker assessed that he was not capable of living alone, even with a full care package. The care staff who had worked with him in the emergency placement disagreed with the social worker, but the latter was supported by her line manager when a review was held. It was obvious when William started attending the group that he was extremely unhappy living in his current residential home. He made many complaints about the home, which Rachel and I passed on to the social worker and we also followed up ourselves. We reached the view that William should be re-assessed, and asked the social worker to attend a session to review the issues with William. But at the end of the session she felt there would be no point in moving him because 'he would never be happy anywhere'. At the time of writing William remains in the same home.

Susan's situation has already been mentioned. When she was experiencing problems in the residential home, options were discussed with her in the group and the leaders liaised closely with her social worker at this time. Susan then transferred to another home.

Finances

The original research project found that many victims needed practical advice about their finances. Similarly in the Beyond Existing groups, problems regarding money were often raised. Members were unsure about accessing their own money or did not understand certain systems (e.g. regarding benefits or payment of fees for residential care).

William frequently became agitated about his financial situation. As with the death of his wife, he had no recollection of how his finances were sorted out when he moved into residential care. This was a very stressful time for him and workers seem to have attempted to minimise the effect the abuse had had on William. When William was admitted to a place of safety he was extremely agitated about his pension and bank books, which the social worker failed to retrieve from his home, to which the abuser still had access. William also found it difficult to grasp the fact that such savings as were left (substantially reduced due to the financial abuse by Edmund) had to pay for his residential care. He became obsessional about his lack of funds and carried his last bank statement around with him. Matters were not helped by the fact that debts had accrued when he was first admitted to care, because payments had not been made to the home. Consequently, £5 was being taken from William's weekly allowance. Much time was spent in group sessions going over the chain of events and presenting the facts to him; positive reinforcement was needed. The group gave William time, which the staff in his home were not able to do. The social worker was invited to attend a session to discuss his placement and also to explain the financial circumstances.

The care staff at the home did not help the situation, as they did not work sufficiently closely with William to help him understand and manage his weekly allowance. When I arrived on one occasion to transport him to the group, William was very upset because he did not have any tobacco and he had no money to buy any. I asked to see the appropriate administrator in charge of the allowance as I knew payment should have been made the day before. We had to wait for 15 minutes to see the relevant member of staff, who then said, 'I gave him his money last night. I don't know what he does with it.' This is not a helpful attitude when a resident has short-term memory loss and needs help with managing his allowance.

Bert talked about his concerns regarding his bank account and lack of money to buy things he needed. This was also an issue for Susan.

Marjorie raised the issue of not having any money at every session. This was a key concern for her when considering whether she should let Jock go into permanent residential care; she knew that her benefits would be reduced. At this point another disclosure came out regarding possible financial abuse. A friend visited 'when it suits her' to transport Marjorie, as she found using public transport difficult with her weight problem. The friend visited her only occasionally but Marjorie was paying her £60 per month. Marjorie said it was a 'definite business arrangement'.

Preparation for death

Bert knew that he was dying when he started attending the Quarry Group. He had participated in the original research project and I was concerned that other professionals were not being honest with him. Bert thought that he was well, the cancer had been dealt with and that he was attending hospital 'just for check-ups'. Care staff were getting mixed messages about how long he had to live. I raised this with the social worker, who eventually asked the consultant to be honest with Bert. The palliative care team then became involved and Bert started attending the group. Being honest and upfront with both Bert and the members was a priority. We introduced one session saying that we wanted to focus on preparing for death and what to do when someone dies. It was not a morbid session at all. Members were very realistic that death was not far away for most of them and talked openly about how they felt about that. None of them, including Bert, were scared. With the exception of Vernon (who said: 'You make your own heaven or you make your own hell'), they all had religious convictions and believed that they would be going to somewhere better. This brought many of them back to talking about the abuse and making the point that life had been very hard. We went on to further discussions about how they coped with bereavement when they lost someone close to them.

Working on the future

In all groups it was important to regularly review members' aspirations. In the first session members had been asked to think about their hopes for the future. This was done in set time frames: 'Where do you want to be physically and emotionally in six months, a year, five years?' This was a way for the leaders to assess the objectives set by members themselves and evaluating the work undertaken (see Chapter 10).

It is hard to measure work with victims of abuse in terms of success and failure, but after evaluating the whole project it is possible to make some comments about members who had worked through the healing process and others who had not.

Quarry Group

As has already been mentioned, Jim and Bert died while the group was running. I would like to think they both got something positive from attending it. The positive work achieved lies with Lilian and Beatrice: Lilian did disclose about all the abuse she had experienced in her life and left the group knowing none of it was her fault and that it is OK to talk about it. It was obvious that she could interact with people (including men) in a more effective way. Beatrice completed the life review she needed to do. The unresolved issues lie with William and Vernon, who are both very unhappy. William is still in the same residential home and Vernon remains living with his wife.

Calder Group

Although Vera did not attend the group regularly, she feels she has healed from the abuse experienced from her husband, but unfortunately she currently has other family problems regarding her two sons. Anna's problems within the residential home continue. Marjorie refused to have contact with the social worker or myself after Jock died. Polly valued attending the two groups but felt frustrated by her inability to get 'justice' for Bert.

Morrison Group

As has already been stated, the Morrison Group continues to run at the time of writing. Edna is one member who has completed the healing process successfully. Susan is working towards healing and with more time she and Hilary will succeed. Vicky has left the group for the moment, but intends to return at some point. She feels there is too much going on in her life to deal with the past abuse at the moment. One might argue she needs to deal with the past in order to deal with the current problems, but it has to be acknowledged that this is not the right time for Vicky to face this. Sharon and Deborah have much more to do. Sharon knows what needs to be done and will do it at her own pace. Deborah is at an early stage of recognising that she is a victim of abuse. The future objective must be to offer her options. Sadly, Kathleen remains in hospital.

CHAPTER 8

Vera's Poems

In previous chapters reference has been made to the fact that Vera wrote regularly in her journal. She wrote about how she felt but she also wrote poetry. What follows is a selection of poetry she read to the Calder Group.

Peace at last

Now at last I am on my own,
Gone are the cruel times I have known.
Why did I stay in a man made hell,
Knowing the man who made it very well.
A gambler, a womaniser, a wife beater too
Never a husband or father that is true.
Now I have freedom in abundance it's said,
But nobody now shares my life or my bed.

I can do all the things I wanted to do,
Without asking if I am allowed to.
I could never do that before I was free,
But now all doors are open for me.
Can you imagine how I must feel,
As I wonder, is my freedom so real.

Each day is a time to rejoice,
I listen and hear my own voice.

Never again will I hear him say,
Your place is here so here you stay.
No false promises made these days,
Still having doubts, will come my way.
I keep what promises I do make,
That was his one big mistake.
Caring for others – no not he,
The lack of care almost ended life for me.

A day to remember is when I am free,
The things I hate no longer will be.
No longer will I see that face,
So mean and hateful, in any place.
What I recall then I must forget,
The hurt I felt it lingers yet.
When I think of all the years that passed,
I know they have gone at last.

I feel nothing for one who gave me hell,
And he lied to me – oh so well.
To tell the truth was not his fame,
And named others so they would carry the blame.
He never confessed about his wrongs,
The way he treated me made me strong.
But the life I have now is with peace of mind,
The tension I felt can now unwind.

Don't be fooled by smooth talking liars,
Who promise to fulfil all your desires.
They give you nothing but hurt and pain,
And when taking your life for financial gain.
They can't believe you kept your life,

So you cheated him by not being his wife.
Thought you beat him at his game,
He will try to achieve fame using your name.

My children

Your birthdays come your birthdays go,
But I never forget as you must know.
I wonder how life has passed you by,
And why my babies had to die.
I remind others should they ever forget,
As my memories of you stay with me yet.
It makes me sad on the days I recall,
To remember those days as the saddest of all.

I imagine a daughter so pretty and sweet,
A son still handsome as when I saw you asleep.
Then a room filled with children of my own,
And such a loving welcome each time I came home.
I have missed seeing you age and also grow,
Missing all the pleasure a mother should know.
Oh Helen you're heartache and Michael you're a tear,
My children I never knew you're far and yet so near.

Remembering is easy forgetting is hard to do,
Some say forget the past oh if only they knew.
If they had known the sorrow I could not share,
Or the tears I shed because of utter despair.
Others think to lose a child is nothing,
There is something they should know.
A child is a life a part of you to hold,
Someone to love and cherish as you're growing old.

The meeting

I know a place of eternal peace and rest,
Where you cannot be awakened from what is blest.
Eternal life with those you knew and loved,
Who went before you with angels and doves.
A place of heavenly peace and joy,
Where I will see my baby girls and boys.
They will have grown into women and men by now,
To recognise them the question is how.

Fair and dark hair framing shining faces,
No thought of people or distant places.
Of a mother who never forgets you in time,
Who has often imagined to be given a sign.
That you remember and come home for a while,
Just to say hello and appear in a recognised style.
You're not forgotten and never will,
I know you're my children and could my life fulfil.

Hope is a thought and a prayer,
An awareness that no others can share.
A dream of what could have been,
But was a life I have never seen.
Taken from love and constant care,
Like a nightmare of which you're unaware.
But others will share and care for you,
And give you the care until my time is through.

Your children

When grown up and men by name,
Your children bring you constant pain.
They wander far and some stay near,
Cause you to cry or bring you cheer.
Your children are your pride and joy,
Sweet gentle girls and tough robust boys.
The parents the same can be said of you,
You cause your children pain and grief too.

Your children will have children too someday,
Then you're grandparents old and frail.
Life itself is passing you by,
You greet each day with a welcome sigh.
We all grow old in age and time,
On this mountain of learning we must climb.
We learn from life the error of our ways,
Some stay on the straights while others stray.

Then as the years will fade away,
Time is lost in deathly grey.
Summers are short the winters long,
The birds now whisper their happy song.
Things now change before your eyes,
Wrinkled faces and darkened skies.
Life itself will leave and depart,
But your children have memories of you in their
    hearts.

Thoughts

Hate I know you oh so well,
What I feel I will now tell.
Wishing each day would be the last,
To be forgotten and left in the past.
A heavy feeling in every room,
That presence makes depressing gloom.
Being left in silence with no care,
Surrounds me with utter despair.
It is well I hate for it makes me strong,
To face each day as it comes along.
I wish and pray to be released,
To be free of the hate and the conceit.
In peace and alone I could happily dwell,
Away from this immoral hateful hell.

Loneliness

All alone in age and time,
Old and feeble yet so refined.
Nobody cares should I live or die,
As to the outside world I cry.
If only someone would visit me,
To have a chat and a cup of tea.
And end the silence in my room,
By brightening the ever constant gloom.
I may not know this present life,
But I have known sorrow and strife.
The winters now are cold and long,
I may not hear the spring birds' song.
My hair is grey and wrinkled face,
Youth has gone and will not be replaced.
Past memories are now growing dim,

As day fades out and night creeps in.
So come yourself my plight to see,
Someday you could be alone like me.

A time to relent

When I die and go to heaven above,
I will look down on those I once loved.
Curse some for the way I bore pain,
Others I will haunt until we meet again.
The times I struggled to do what I could,
Never asking for favours as sick people would.
They spurned me and left me to suffer alone,
A home became a prison from which I have flown.

Always doing as others would bid me do,
They used and abused me the stronger few.
Orders must be obeyed without denial,
Leave your sick-bed to please is final.
I have power in death to stop all the rules,
Now I am the one laughing at the mean fools.
They used me in life as a slave but no more,
For I will be free now and of that I am sure.

When you're sick some don't understand,
They act ignorant of how illness is planned.
Is suffering for others not seen or felt,
But taken for granted as they relent.
Too late they feel what they did was wrong,
If this is the word they will use to make them strong.
Yet if they had treated the sick person right,
They would not be sitting alone tonight.

Untitled

What can life offer me but strife,
No devotion as a mother no love as a wife.
An object of abuse whose life has no meaning,
Cook and bottle washer doing washing and cleaning.
Someone living on borrowed time without care,
Caught like a timid animal in a deathly snare.
Man is my killer being thoughtless and cruel,
Measuring my life the one they would rule.

Fetch bring and carry do as they say,
Makes me a servant in every way.
Tired and ill a fact they ignore,
Treat me as an object a perpetual bore.
I feel I must travel and go on my way,
Leave this place and go astray.
Pain and heartache all suffered in vain,
A feeling of loss and resentment remain.

My needs are ignored not part of life,
Still voices tell me that is rife.
What I gave is thought of as just right,
Not their worry but my own plight.
Misery surrounds me life hard to bear,
Alone in my suffering of this I'm aware.
Wrapped in depression not wanted I'm sure,
Life has nothing but death is a cure.

'Piper Alpha' memorium

Pain and death in a deep black sea,
It will not release or set them free.
Like a cradle it rocks you to and fro,
In the deepest sleep you will ever know.
The tears of sorrow being shed,
Are for the lost and lonely dead.
Voices cry out but utter no sound,
As they wait in the depths to be found.

The sea is filled with sorrow and grief,
Restless souls lost in the deep.
That fatal day when life was lost,
In fire and smoke in explosions tossed.
The sea beneath the oil rig of doom,
Is filled with death and solitary gloom.
An empty space in each man's home,
For a place beneath the briney foam.

Loved ones wait to lay them to rest,
Away from the watery wooden chest.
Remember how they left to toil,
Some for gas and others for oil.
They will never leave your side,
But now with 'God' they must abide.
They look down from up above,
And still watch over those they love.

Memorium to a miner

A young man to a mine did go,
Will he return we do not know.
The sky is not above his head,
But tons of earth as for the dead.

He works in darkness all his life,
A safety lamp his only light.
When danger comes he can but run,
Not knowing when the end will come.

They criticise these courageous men,
If not by words then by the pen.
A miner's life is far from fun,
He is tired and weary when day is done.
The day will come we all well know,
When death will come as life must go.
But must it be where none can see,
They wait in death to be set free.

So remember the toil and strife,
These men endured to give us light.
Their courage makes our fires burn bright,
To warm us on cold winter nights.
God in his mercy I know will say,
With me you now must always stay.
The sorrow and the tears now shed,
Are for the living of the dead.

For they will see an empty chair,
No longer their loved ones seated there.
And when you feel you're not alone,
Don't be afraid they have come home.
You feel a gentle breeze pass by,
Sounding like a distant sigh.
Grief makes heavy a loving heart,
But love lives on though death us do part.

CHAPTER 9

Problems and Lessons Learnt

Some of the problems encountered in running the groups have been mentioned in previous chapters. When Beyond Existing was set up, one of the objectives was to test out different ways of working (e.g. running mixed and single gender groups; having one or two leaders facilitating; having the groups running at different times of day). The purpose of this chapter is to summarise the main difficulties and to expand on some of them, so that anyone who is considering setting up a support group for abused people might be forewarned about what to expect. The chapter will address very practical problems and also more professional issues regarding working with victims of abuse.

Resources

Beyond Existing was set up with a very small initial budget of £1,000 and securing more funding was time-consuming and problematic. The project was successful in that it achieved its main objectives as set out in the mission statement. In a time when resources are tight and applying for funding requires specialist skills, the success of this project indicates that much can be achieved on a small budget and that human resources are as important as financial resources.

Funding

Beyond Existing was fortunate in the beginning because it was set up with funding from the Joseph Rowntree Foundation. It was when we started to make grant applications that it became obvious we were going to find it difficult to secure further funding. Applying for funding is a skill and nowadays there are training courses available to develop the necessary skills; there are also people who can give advice about making applications. It is useful to contact the local voluntary action service in the first instance. People proposing to set up groups which will need to secure funding need to acquire the knowledge and skills regarding grant applications, otherwise a lot of time can be wasted. One also has to be realistic that preparing any grant application does take a considerable amount of time.

Our applications were not complex. The people who were involved in Beyond Existing gave their time voluntarily, so we were not making applications for paid workers. We were asking for funding for very basic things; for example:

- stationery

- stamps

- leaflets

- posters

- publicity costs

- transport (taxis for victims to get to and from the sessions).

It was a struggle to get funding, even though we were asking for small amounts. We concluded that older people are still not seen to have any priority and are therefore very much excluded and marginalised. Although the subject of elder abuse is gaining more recognition, it seems it is still not an emotive issue for the public – unlike child abuse and domestic violence.

Beyond Existing received donations in kind from Churchtown Social Services Department. Again it was fortunate that links had already been made because of the previous research project. New groups may have to undertake a lot of groundwork in order to gain similar support. It was incredibly helpful to Beyond Existing that the Department provided venues free of charge, as well as allowing a worker to co-facilitate two of the groups. Internal mail systems were also used to publicise the groups.

Publicity

In Chapter 2 details were given about how Beyond Existing was publicised; it was also stated that the response overall was disappointing. With hindsight it is difficult to know what could have been done differently, as all relevant bodies within the statutory, voluntary and private sectors were informed about Beyond Existing's activities. An objective was for the leaflets and posters to be eye-catching, as it is a known fact that workers in all sectors have too much paper arriving on their desks (see Appendices for examples of leaflets and posters). Perhaps one of the lessons learnt was that the majority of telephone enquiries came from people who had seen the posters in local post offices, which are obviously still an important meeting place for older people.

These responses also gave a clear indication that there is a need for some kind of information/advice line on a local level.

Many organisations have helplines (e.g. Action on Elder Abuse) but people often want to ring somewhere in their own local area. With the introduction of *No Secrets* in March 2000, it was expected that by October 2001 every area in the UK would have in place a multi-agency policy and procedure on adult abuse and all workers should be receiving basic awareness training on this subject (Department of Health 2000). The telephone enquiries received from workers (mainly home carers and residential staff) were mainly about how to report abuse; that is, who to report to. It is a concern that workers are still not aware of correct procedures.

The telephone enquiries from the general public also indicated that people are unsure what to do about abuse and violence to older people. The situation is comparable to over twenty years ago, where there was persistent unawareness about child abuse and domestic violence.

Attitude/referrals

Because of the amount of effort that went into publicising Beyond Existing, it was surprising that more referrals were not received from social services staff. Information about the groups went out each month with the monitoring form from the Adult Abuse and Protection Project. I often followed up cases through the project and contacted social workers to talk to them about an individual case, and also to enquire whether they thought the alleged victim might benefit from some groupwork. There was a great reluctance to suggest the idea to victims. It is difficult to know exactly why this was, but from conversations which took place the reluctance stemmed from:

- the worker having closed the case even if there were long-term needs outstanding

- not understanding the value of groupwork

- feeling that the leaders might open up issues the social worker had not dealt with

- lack of thought given to how multi-agency working may provide for long-term work.

In a time when social workers spend most of their time undertaking assessments and doing little long-term work, surely a resource such as Beyond Existing should be utilised. It has been acknowledged that groupwork is not for everybody, but the option of attending a support group should be offered to victims. Social workers must be more proactive (and less precious) about using resources in the voluntary sector to meet the needs of adults. It is a problem of attitude, and work needs to be done to change this if people are to truly work in partnership.

It has to be said that not all social workers were unresponsive. A pattern which developed was that certain social services staff did keep details about Beyond Existing, and these were the workers who made referrals. In some cases, on making contact, victims decided that they did not wish to attend.

Commitment

All the people involved with Beyond Existing were very committed to the project and gave their time on a voluntary basis; this included members of the advisory group, group leaders, and staff within Churchtown Social Services Department. Supporters of such a project need to feel passionately about the work to be undertaken. Struggling for resources as well as dealing with disclosures can be emotionally draining; it is important to have people supporting the work who can maintain enthusiasm and encouragement during the difficult times. An advisory group can also offer practical advice and monitor the activities, which is part of a good evaluation process.

Time

Organising groups takes an enormous amount of time and this should never be underestimated. It is an important consideration for workers who are thinking of running groups as part of their normal job. Planning needs to take place in the early stages in relation to what can and will be offered to group members. Setting objectives and developing a mission statement are imperative preliminaries before publicising a group and its activities. Meetings need to be organised between advisers, funders and leaders. Once a start date has been set for a group, more time needs to be allocated by the leaders to visit potential members and then to plan the sessions. What we grossly underestimated was the amount of time taken up after the groups started running – for example, we did not anticipate the time spent on supporting members between sessions, liaising with agencies and professionals, responding to telephone enquiries and administrative issues.

Skills and knowledge

Workers can be trained to become groupworkers, and workers who have not had such training should not be deterred from becoming involved in a group, provided some preparation and support are available. Many workers will be 'natural' groupworkers. Rachel had some experience of working in groups but was worried about 'not being experienced enough' for Beyond Existing. In fact she had a lot of experience regarding abuse; her previous and current jobs had involved working with older people who had been abused and she had been closely involved with the original research project. All she lacked was self-confidence.

Rachel did a lot of reading to prepare herself, and she talked to me. We were careful to plan how she would take more of a lead as the Quarry Group developed. We also planned what we would do if certain situations occurred (although one can never plan for every eventuality). During the two years since we started, Rachel has developed her groupwork skills, gained confidence and 'learnt a lot'. This has been shown in the way she now participates in the Morrison Group; I have witnessed how she is much more relaxed, more interactive with members, and willingly takes the lead in facilitating the group.

Having some knowledge and understanding about abuse and being able to handle disclosures is a fundamental require-ment in groupwork with survivors. If a group is being run for older people who are victims of elder abuse, it is important to have some knowledge about child abuse and domestic violence as well. As previous studies (Pritchard 2000, 2001) and Beyond Existing have found, older people may have been abused earlier in life, and this may have to be dealt with in the group. A leader has to have the skills to respond appropriately and offer the necessary support. There will be times when a leader might be shocked or surprised; Rachel certainly experi-enced this when hearing some disclosures about child abuse. Again, she had prepared herself through reading about adult survivors of child abuse, but hearing about the reality of abuse from members themselves can still be very upsetting. Rachel coped very well indeed; she kept her reactions within herself until after the session had finished. Debriefing and supervision sessions were very important for her to learn from these experi-ences.

Leaders' emotions

Leaders have to work in a professional way in order to support the members. Rachel openly talked about her worries about controlling her own emotions. Being involved in the groups was a new experience and one which she wanted to pursue for her own personal and professional development. She rightly anticipated that she might become over-involved emotionally in the groups when disclosures were made. We discussed what was appropriate behaviour and what was not; then developed strategies to deal with such situations. There were occasions early on when Rachel became very tearful and, as agreed, she left the group when this happened. When discussing ground rules it had been agreed that *anyone* (members or leaders) could leave the room if they needed to.

If someone is new to groupwork or dealing with abuse, it is important to discuss what could happen before the sessions begin. Nobody is expected to behave like a robot; we are all human and will react to what we hear. It takes time to learn to deal with one's feelings. This is where debriefing and supervision can be so important as part of one's professional development. Skills have to be developed to deal with what is heard in the sessions, and also to be able to 'cut off' from what has been worked on after the sessions have finished.

No matter how experienced you are, sometimes certain things will still affect you, so that you find it hard to control your emotions and set your thoughts aside later in the day. All my working life is currently linked to dealing with abuse and I like to think I can deal with most situations which are presented to me. However, I am not ashamed to admit that I too struggled with my emotions at times during some sessions and I think this demonstrates that, as workers, we need to remind ourselves that we will be affected by what we hear. I can control my emotions in the work situation and did so in the sessions;

however, on occasions it was very necessary for me to have a good cry afterwards. I was moved by some of the writing in journals which members read out, and particularly by Vera's poetry (see Chapter 8).

One leader or two?

One aim for Beyond Existing was to test out different ways of working; these included facilitating a group with just one leader. The Calder Group was run by me alone, and it worked satisfactorily only because it was a small group (never more than four members at a session) and no problems occurred during the sessions. By that I mean it would have been difficult if a member had needed time out from the group or if a member had not been able to relate to me (which sometimes does happen in groupwork). In other words, members' choices were limited. I would conclude that it is preferable to have two leaders, but when resources are really stretched and two workers cannot be released (perhaps in a residential or day care setting) it is worth trying to run a group with one leader. It is helpful to discuss the issue with members so that they know that if a member needs to be alone with the leader during the session, then there may be additional unplanned breaks in the session for that period.

The other problem which arises when having only one leader is the lack of support. I was very fortunate in that I had good working relationships with the manager and staff at the Calder Centre. More often than not, the manager was around after the session had finished and it was good to be able to wind down by having a general chat, rather than getting straight into the car and driving home. Obviously this was not proper debriefing because I could not break confidentiality and talk about issues related to the group, except where a member was known to the Calder Centre and an agreement had been reached about sharing information.

I did have an added safety net in that an outside consultant was working for the research project to give me independent support; had anything arisen in the Calder Group, I could have used this person as an emergency contact. So this is another important point to make for anyone who is considering running a group alone; a person must be identified who is willing to debrief and support the leader.

Cancelling sessions

A problem which arose for us on several occasions, and which may happen to other leaders, is when a leader cannot attend the group. We always arranged dates of sessions to avoid planned holidays, but there were occasions when Rachel was instructed by senior management that she had to attend emergency meetings within her department, so I was left to run the groups (Quarry and Morrison) alone at very short notice. This is another matter which leaders need to plan for in advance of the situation arising. They need to be honest about whether they have the skills and confidence to run a group alone or, if a decision is made to cancel the meeting, how members will be informed about this.

We only had to cancel one session at short notice and this was because none of the members of the Morrison Group (except Susan) could attend. Telephone calls were made and formal letters of apology sent out. We received feedback from Susan's social worker about the devastating effect this had had on Susan because she so looks forward to the sessions. It was impossible to arrange a session earlier than the next one planned a month ahead.

Time of day

Another thing that was tested out was the time of day when groups were run, and also what it is was like for a leader to run two groups back to back in one day. The Quarry Group ran in the morning (10.00 a.m. until midday) and the Calder Group ran in the afternoon (3.00 p.m. to 5.00 p.m.). In the pilot study they ran back to back, so that I was often involved with members until after they had had their lunch at the Quarry Centre, and once they left, I left for the Calder Centre. On average I had about an hour to unwind from the Quarry Centre and 'psych' myself up for the Calder Group, but this vital time included travelling across the city. The Morrison Group met at different times, either in the morning (10.00 a.m. to midday), over lunchtime (12.00 to 2.00 p.m.) or in the afternoon (2.30 to 4.30 p.m.).

From the leaders' point of view, morning sessions were better – purely because we did not get pulled into dealing with other aspects of our jobs before the sessions started. The members did not seem to have any preferences. Members of the Calder Group liked the afternoon because, as one member said, 'it gives me something to look forward to'. The women often complained that 'days seemed very long', stemming from the fact that they felt very alone.

I found running two groups in one day very exhausting emotionally and would not recommend anyone to do this. In the pilot study, it had been decided to test this out because of constraints on staff time. If an organisation is going to run two groups on different days, the time involved will eat into more than two half-days and it can be more cost-effective to work one long day. However, the quality of work may well be ad-versely affected. I know in some of the Calder Group sessions I was not as quick-witted as I would have wished and found it hard to keep my concentration; my note-taking was not as good, and my recall at a later time was adversely affected.

Venue

In Chapter 2 suggestions were made about finding a good venue. The main problem Beyond Existing faced was at the Quarry Centre, where staff sometimes interrupted the sessions. This was because they saw people they knew in the group or they wanted to speak to their colleague, Rachel. The location of the room probably contributed to this problem because it was on the ground floor and had a glass door. Also it was normally used as one of the main lounges, so sometimes staff came in looking for residents, forgetting that a Beyond Existing Group had been booked in the room. Even though Rachel discussed this problem at the centre's staff meetings it took a long time for staff to understand the importance of privacy. By the time the Morrison Group was set up in the same location, all the problems had been resolved.

The Calder Group used a small room on the first floor of the Calder Centre. This was out of the way and not normally used very much by residents, so there were no interruptions.

Effect on other service users

Leaders also have to be mindful of any possible harm (physical or emotional) to other service users in a centre where a group is meeting. For example, Lilian's behaviour could be extremely difficult and challenging; she would become very agitated, and refuse to walk if other service users came near her when on her way to the meeting room. There were also problems in the dining room when she stayed for lunch. If any men came near her, she would become disruptive; so care had to be taken about where she sat. She would occasionally swear or make inappropriate comments, which could be quite frightening to other people. Because of confidentiality, it was not possible to explain to other people why she behaved in this way. Time was taken with Lilian to talk about the effect her behaviour would have on other people – service users, visitors and staff.

Health and safety issues

One emotion which may present itself among group members (and leaders) during the sessions is fear, and leaders need to consider health and safety issues affected by this. Some members have the potential to be violent. If such a person becomes angry when disclosing information about abuse, then leaders must have strategies in place to protect members and themselves, should an outburst occur. People in the building should be aware that, if an alarm is used, an immediate response is required. One member in the Morrison Group had a history of violent behaviour; she was very honest about this. If she had given any indication that she was going to attack anyone in the group she would have been asked to leave the group permanently.

Not everyone will be honest about their tendency to violent behaviour. Therefore, when screening potential members, leaders should gather as much information as possible about the person's likely response to stress. The leaders have a responsibility for the safety of others and for themselves.

The venues used to run the groups were not publicised, because some members were still living in abusive situations and it was important to protect them from visits from their abusers. The importance of maintaining privacy has already been mentioned, but a related problem was to ensure that staff within the centres did not disclose that Beyond Existing met in the centres. In fact, some staff did talk about Beyond Existing's activities without thinking, and steps had to be taken to ensure that they realised that confidentiality had to be maintained in order to promote safety.

Transport

Arranging transport was one of our biggest practical problems in running the groups. The lesson learnt is that leaders need to allocate enough time to deal with transport issues – whether they are actually transporting members themselves or booking taxis.

We had underestimated the amount of funding we would need for transport. This was because we had not envisaged that such large distances would be travelled by some members and that they would require transport. We had originally hoped that when a member had a social worker already involved, s/he might provide transport to the sessions. Some social workers were willing to do this, but others absolutely refused, saying they did not have the time.

It is necessary to emphasise the importance of victims feeling safe when being transported to a session. If taxis are used, it is important to use a reliable firm which understands that difficulties may arise with some of the people being transported. The members need to feel safe with the drivers.

Rachel found it an added pressure transporting some of the members to the Quarry Group. She became frustrated that residential staff were hindering what should have been a simple task: Beatrice and Lilian were rarely ready to come when Rachel arrived at the pre-arranged time to collect them.

Other problems arose when social workers made arrangements for workers from other agencies (e.g. private home carers; residential staff) to transport members to the sessions.

Messages were often received to say that a member would not be attending; messages like this were always followed up immediately and the usual reason given was that staff were not available to meet the agreement. Luckily, we usually found out at least the day before the session was due to take place, so alternative arrangements could be made. In some cases it was necessary to make new arrangements and to use taxis on a regular basis, which was an unexpected additional expense for the project.

Frequency of sessions

We would have liked to have run a group which met weekly for a period of two months, but did not have the resources to do this. Therefore, it is not possible to discuss whether more frequent sessions would have made a difference to the outcomes achieved. However, views about frequency can be ascertained from leaders and members. The majority of members said that they liked the sessions to be held monthly; they indeed seemed to cope with the time gap better than the leaders did. I personally felt frustrated, as I would have liked to have seen members more regularly in order to avoid a feeling of discontinuity. Very often, explanations about the work being undertaken or issues recently discussed had to be repeated, and this might not have occurred so often, had the groups met more frequently.

On the positive side, each group ran for approximately twelve months, during which time members could build trusting relationships with each other and with the leaders. The advantage of having a group which runs for a considerable length of time is that members do not feel forced to enter into relationships too quickly. Some members also commented that they knew the group was 'there for them'. Even though the ground rules enjoined regular attendance from members, they understood that with an open group it was possible to come and go without losing membership. At certain times, some members feel that they want to be on their own and not to engage with other people, and it is important to respect this.

Gender issues

Beyond Existing showed that older men and women can work together successfully in a group setting. It initially seemed rather radical to propose a group which included both male and female victims of sexual abuse; groups for survivors usually are single sex. In other words, gender is usually discussed in relation to the leaders rather than the membership. One normally thinks of women working with female survivors and men working with male survivors. The work undertaken in the Quarry Group suggests that one should not make assumptions about gender (at least when working with older people), but rather that potential members of a group should be asked if they have any preferences or problems in regard to the gender of the leaders and members. Ideally they should be offered a choice, but with restricted resources this is unlikely. The members in the Quarry Group who had been sexually abused expressed no preferences, and once they were ready to disclose their experiences they could talk about sexual abuse openly with people of the opposite sex. This would not be possible for all victims, however; one male victim who wanted to attend a group decided not to, as he felt he needed two male leaders, which we could not provide at that time. We hope to do so in the future.

Age and disability

Originally Beyond Existing had been set up to work with older people; but in Stage 3 younger adults with mental health problems and learning disabilities were referred, so that the Morrison Group included adults from 39 years of age upwards. Again, because of the success of this, one could argue that agencies should be promoting groupwork across the specialisms (that is, across the range of service user groups). It is possible for younger and older people to communicate effectively and support each other. There may be many benefits for service users from different specialisms to meet with each other; obviously there has to be some common ground, and in the case of Beyond Existing this was the shared experience of having been abused.

Levels of mental capacity and capabilities

The three groups were very different in the way they worked. There were similarities in the issues addressed, but the way in which the work was carried out varied. This was due largely to differences in members' mental capacity and capabilities.

The Quarry Group went at a very slow pace and there was much repetition between sessions, because some members had difficulty in communicating. Vernon and Beatrice had hearing problems; Lilian had had a stroke which affected her speech; William had short-term memory problems. It was possible to work with all the members but a lot of time, patience and co-operation from all members was required.

The Calder Group had no such problems. All the women had full mental capacity. The only disadvantage was that owing to ill-health some of them had erratic attendance, so work was impeded.

The only person with communication difficulties in the Morrison Group was Kathleen. She had a speech impediment and it was very difficult to understand her; but everyone was very supportive and patient. Deborah was shy, but could communicate well. She sometimes repeated things, but again, members were patient and the leaders could move her on when appropriate.

People who do not have full mental capacity should not be excluded from groupwork. Some members had memory problems which did affect the pace at which work was undertaken, but it did not make it impossible. Members need to be able to say openly if they have a problem with another member in a group; the facility to do this in private should be offered so as not to give offence. If this ground rule had been in place, maybe Vernon would have been able to express his difficulties with William earlier rather than in the evaluation questionnaire (see following chapter on evaluation).

Health problems

Members of the groups had health problems which affected the running of the groups. Ill-health caused attendance problems particularly for the Calder Group, whose members were frequently either ill or had to attend hospital appointments. This eventually resulted in the group having to be terminated.

Continence problems can occur when people become stressed or upset. This certainly happened to members in the Quarry Group. So it is important to have planned breaks as well as aids readily available – that is, continence pads, change of clothing, etc.

Working with residential/nursing homes

Some of the problems which arose with residential and nursing homes have already been mentioned, but it will be useful to be explicit about the exact nature of the problems at this time when there is great emphasis from the Government on the importance of 'working in partnership'.

For members living in permanent care, the residential/nursing homes were regularly sent lists of dates for future sessions. They were also contacted the day before each session as a reminder that a worker would be collecting the member, or that a taxi would be booked. Despite these arrangements, members were often not ready to leave on time.

The work which was being undertaken by Beyond Existing should properly have been written into the members' care plans, but it was evident that details were not included. Some homes seemed to be deliberately obstructive. In William's case, the home had a minibus for residents but the manager would not agree to it being used for William; instead she offered to book a taxi from their end to make it cheaper one way. However, the home failed to do this and after William missed a session, I took responsibility for picking him up and he did not miss any more sessions. Nevertheless, when evaluating the Quarry Group after it had finished, the activities officer wrote on William's evaluation form: '...at the time he got very agitated as the transport was not very reliable in collecting William so consequently he didn't attend many of your sessions.'

The homes complained about the sessions ending around midday and the fact that the members might not return until 1.00 p.m. when lunch would have been finished. Obviously this should not have been a problem, but it seemed that it was in some cases – so much so, that the manager of the Quarry

Centre offered to provide lunch for the members after the session had finished.

Certain problems arose for members which Rachel and I as leaders felt needed to be taken up with the individual homes. Some issues were resolved, others were not, and we had to take these matters further. Beatrice came to the sessions either with only one hearing aid (she wore hearing aids in both ears), or the batteries were not working. This seriously hindered communication in the group. Rachel raised this issue with staff in the home every time she returned Beatrice from the group. Beatrice's hearing needed a reassessment, as did her eyesight. Neither assessment took place in the twelve months of our working together.

Lilian always came to the sessions in her slippers, which were dangerous. The sole on each slipper was torn and she could easily have tripped. Again, the home was alerted but nothing happened. Lilian also came in very dirty, old clothes. We questioned what was happening to her personal allowance and whether she was taken shopping.

William also came in very dirty clothes. This was resolved because we eventually contacted the social worker after being told by the home that William's personal allowance was paying his arrears. The social worker made an application to the coal miners' welfare association and obtained a special grant which enabled William to buy a whole new wardrobe of clothes. Other problems for William related to his not having had breakfast when he arrived at the session; not having his walking stick, pipe or tobacco. When he did have the walking stick it was usually covered in dirt and unknown substances.

The problems regarding Susan's situation in the first residential home have been mentioned earlier. Her emotional needs were being neglected. She had no stimulation at all and was kept within the building. Her social worker was very active on the case and we liaised closely with her.

What is worrying about all of these cases is that staff within the homes should have dealt with these matters so that they did not arise in the first place. Personal care was not given adequate attention and this is why we had to take matters further. We raised these problems with social workers in the first instance and then with registration and inspection officers.

Knowing when to finish

One of the dangers of groupwork is that it can create dependency. Beyond Existing aimed to promote the well-being of its members and to improve their quality of life, not to encourage reliance on the group for support indefinitely. At the outset it is important to talk about time-limits if they are to be in place. At the beginning of the pilot study it was made clear that the groups were being set up as an experiment for six months. When members of the Quarry Group were reminded about this four months in, it was evident that they felt very threatened by the possible loss.

Beyond Existing has been constrained at each stage by funding limitations. It was fortunate that we secured more funding in order to continue, as one can never predict how long it will take a person to heal from abuse. The whole healing process could take years rather than months, and in an ideal world a group run for abused adults should be open and able to continue until the healing is complete. Unfortunately we do not live in an ideal world, so when such groups are run it has to be the leaders' responsibility to ensure proper closure.

The Quarry Group continued for a further six months when funding was secured (as did the Calder Group), by which time it was clear that we had done all the necessary work.

However, two months before the end, when we started the 'ending' work, members were upset. They had come to rely on the group as a social event. In order to try to keep the group going, Lilian started repeating things which had been worked through.

As stated earlier, the Calder Group finished earlier than planned because of members' ill-health, and the Morrison Group is still running at the time of writing. When an open group is continuing to run, there may be situations where a member has 'healed' but wants to remain in the group. This has happened in the case of Edna in the Morrison Group. She feels she still benefits from attending the group but in fact it is other members who gain from Edna and her experience of the healing process, which she shares with new members. She has become a role model for the group.

CHAPTER 10

Evaluation

Evaluation should be undertaken regularly when organising and running groups. It is vital to get everyone's perspective – that is, to give participants the opportunity to voice their opinions about how the group is functioning and whether it is meeting their needs and helping them to achieve their objectives. Evaluation is also an important part of ending a group. Evaluation can be formal or informal; whatever methods are adopted, there are difficulties regarding objectivity and measuring success. Brown comments:

> Objective evaluation of groupwork effectiveness is difficult to achieve because of the complexity of the variables and problems of accurate measurement... This should not deter the groupworker from rough-and-ready methods which obtain some useful information for future planning and agency policy. (Brown 1994, p.198)

Evaluation was undertaken regularly in all three Beyond Existing groups. This was achieved by:

- evaluating the work undertaken at the end of each session

- putting evaluation as an item on the agenda every six months

- evaluation at final session

- written questionnaires sent to members three months after the group had finished.

Monthly evaluation

The importance of evaluation was explained to members in each group; it was made clear that leaders needed to know what was helpful and not helpful to members in order that the group could meet their needs.

At each session there were certain standing agenda items, one of which was regarding the ending of each session. It was important to check out how members were feeling and also to evaluate what in their view had been achieved, and what they liked or disliked in the manner and content of the work.

Six-month evaluation

The pilot study (Stage 1) was intended to run for six months. By that time it had become clear from what members were saying in the Quarry and Calder Groups that they wanted to continue; also it was evident to the leaders that a lot more work needed to be undertaken regarding the healing process. It was necessary to remind members of the original objective; that is, for them to have the opportunity to talk about the abuse they had experienced and deal with issues surrounding that abuse. The leaders could see that the Quarry Group might be in danger of becoming just a social occasion for some of the members. So the leaders were determined to ensure that the group was re-evaluated and members were clear about the purpose of the group.

It was felt that part of a session should be devoted to evaluating the groups. This was done through group discussion. The members did not need much encouragement to voice their views but the following questions were put to them:

1. What have you got out of the group?

2. What has been useful?

3. What has not been useful?

4. What do you like about the group?

5. What don't you like about the group?

6. Can we [the leader(s)] do anything else to help you?

7. What do you need to do in the future?

8. Is there anything else you would like to say?

All the comments were very positive and some of them were used as direct quotes when the Beyond Existing leaflets were redesigned:

- You get introduced to everyone and everyone gets to know you.

- You can talk in here. Nowhere else will they listen to you.

- I've gained knowledge.

- You've always got someone to back you up.

- I feel very comfortable, safe in this group.

- Nice people – makes a difference.

- Everyone is nice to me.
- It's better talking than bottling it up all the time.

Endings

It is important to end groupwork properly; that is, there should be a proper winding down period and people should go away from the group knowing what they have achieved. Although it may be painful, people should say their goodbyes.

The final session should also involve an evaluation. It was not possible for the Calder Group to have a proper ending as the group came to end because members could no longer attend due to ill-health and other personal circumstances.

The Quarry Group voiced similar comments to what has been said above. When they knew that the group was going to end, some started raising issues which had been dealt with. It was clear that they did not want the group to finish. Lilian in particular found it very hard; she started crying and became very agitated. Rachel took her out of the group to deal with this. Perhaps one of the most important comments came from Lilian at the end, which indicated that the sessions did have an ongoing impact: 'I enjoy the group and think about everyone and what they have said when I get home.'

From discussions which took place it was clear that the group had achieved the following for its members:

- the opportunity to talk
- support to face the abuse which has happened
- a feeling of safety
- company
- a sense of belonging

- advice

- support.

Beatrice: I feel comfortable. I feel like I belong. I take a bit of grasping. I like people. I can tell straight away if they are going to be nice.

Lilian: To meet people. I've enjoyed coming here. I've been able to talk.

Three months after closure

It is usually helpful for a person to reflect back on an event after it has finished in order to realise what impact there has been. So three months after the Quarry and Calder Groups had finished, a questionnaire (reproduced below) was designed for evaluation purposes. This was sent to all members in both groups with a letter of explanation. Letters were also sent to the residential/nursing homes asking staff to help the members with the questionnaires if necessary. William's home returned the questionnaire uncompleted, saying that he could not remember the group and 'the transport was not very reliable in collecting William so consequently he didn't attend many of your sessions'. This was completely untrue; the only time he had not attended was when the home forgot to book the taxis and at that point I started collecting him. From then on he attended regularly. It goes to show that we are all at risk of re-constructing the past to suit our own needs and prejudices! Even professionals do not escape this kind of human folly.

Beyond Existing
Questionnaire

Name: .... Date of birth: ....

Address: ....

Tel. No.: .... Group attended: ....

1. What were your expectations of the group before you came to the first meeting?

2. Was it different to what you expected? If it was, how was it different?

3. What did you gain from attending the group?

4. What was helpful to you?

5. What was not helpful?

6. Was there anything else you needed in the group?
   (e.g. specific help, advice, subject for discussion)

7. What do you think was helpful to other members
   of the group?

8. If you attended another group in the future, would
   you want anything to be changed/done
   differently?

9. Please write down any other thoughts you have
   regarding what was good or bad about your
   experience of attending the group.

10. Have you any other suggestions for groups which
    are run in the future?

11. If another group ran would you prefer the group to meet:

   (a)   monthly for six months?

   (b)   every two weeks for three months?

   (c)   every week for two months?

12. Please make any comments you have on the following:

   Transport arrangements for getting to the group:

   The location of the meeting:

   The meeting room:

   Refreshments:

13. Overall, how useful did you find the group on a scale 1 to 10 (1 being not at all; 10 being very useful)?

**THANK YOU FOR TAKING TIME TO
COMPLETE THIS QUESTIONNAIRE**

**Please return the questionnaire in the stamped
addressed envelope provided**

Marjorie was the only person not to return the questionnaire. Some members gave detailed responses; others only answered some questions. The majority were positive, but Vernon gave negative responses to each question. Rachel and I were very concerned at what he had written, in particular:

'I felt I did not gain anything from attending the group.'

'I thought they talked to another person all the time and not enough to me.'

'They did not give me advice on how to get into residential care so that I could get away from my wife.'

Rachel and I discussed all Vernon's comments, which came as a real shock, and we decided that Rachel should talk to him the next time he attended for day care. We felt it was important to understand why he felt this way. She did so with a day care worker present, whom Vernon likes. Vernon was still negative but it seemed to stem from the fact that he thought William talked and interrupted too much; Vernon felt neglected. Rachel and I discussed this afterwards and concluded that we needed to be more observant in the future. We thought we had managed William, but obviously not enough. We also learnt that Vernon did not feel he could express this in the group. We had been under the misapprehension that he enjoyed talking to William about old times as they knew so many people in common.

Rachel said quite openly to Vernon that she thought the comment about not giving him information about residential care had been unfair. She reminded him that three sessions had been spent on this and that his social worker had attended one session; he said he did not remember this at all. This confirmed our concerns that Vernon was starting to have some memory problems and was presenting as very depressed.

Summary of responses

- **Expectations**

  I was not sure what to expect.

  Expected it to be different.

  Somewhere to go and learn how to cope with stress.

  I was curious about what help I would gain by talking.

  I expected a surpise.

  None.

- **How was it different from expectations?**

  I found it so much easier to talk and explain.

  Yes – you find there are other people who are going through stress in different ways.

  Came to collect me and sat and talked to me about different things.

  At first I was still unsure.

  Same.

- **Gains**

  Confidence.

  I made friends with some people.

  Listening to other people made me realise I was lucky to be as I am.

I found out it was easier to talk to other people than your own family and I am not alone in this world with problems.

The truth about my situation and how wrong I was to accept it as normal.

A lot. That I was a real person and things that happened to me were not my fault.

I felt I did not gain anything from attending the group.

- **What was helpful?**

Expressing my feelings and being helped.

Yes it was a change.

Great, lovely. Very helpful to me. Kind.

I do not think they helped me at all.

- **Not helpful**

Others not opening up and facing the facts then moving forward with confidence.

I thought they talked to another person all the time and not enough to me.

- **Other things needed**

No.

Someone to understand and it was always available.

They did not give me advice on how to get into residential care so I could not get away from my wife.

- **Helpful to other members**

  Talking to other people in the group.

  Everything.

  Being able to talk knowing other members would listen and comment.

  Your counselling.

  There were people in the group that thought it was helpful.

- **Things which could be changed/done differently**

  I would like the welcome and concern to be the same.

  Nothing.

  Yes, I would like to know where I stand on legal matters. This type of information to be given to me and others.

- **Other thoughts about the experience**

  I didn't feel I was in those circumstances.

  I think everything was fine.

  The only thing to interfere with my group attendance was family matters and my health.

  I cannot think of any way you can change your meetings, as I came home with a little more peace of mind.

  Very good.

  I did not really like the group and was glad when it finished.

- **Suggestions for future groups**

  Like to go and air my views.

  It could help some members of groups to be in a house group meeting.

- **Frequency**

Monthly for six months	2
Every two weeks for three months	2
Every week for two months	0

  If they have another group I think I am getting too old for next time.

- **Transport arrangements**

  Very good.

  Good.

- **Location**

  Very good.

  Fine. Very good.

- **Meeting room**

  Good.

  Nice.

- **Refreshments**

  Good.

  Coffee, biscuits very nice.

- **Usefulness** (Score: 1 – not at all; 10 – very useful)

  5

  10

  10 – I found it very useful.

Evaluating the Morrison Group

The Morrison Group has followed the same system of evaluation as the Quarry and Calder Groups; that is, evaluating at the end of each session. Since starting the group, members have been aware that I have been writing this book, and when drawing to the end, four members agreed to complete the evaluation questionnaire which had previously been sent to members of the Quarry and Calder Groups after those groups were terminated. What follows is a summary of their responses:

- **Expectations**

  Scary.

  To talk and tell.

  No idea.

  To be more reassured.

- **How was it different from expectations?**

  Yes – the people were friendly.

- **Gains**

  A lot. That I was a real person and things that happened to me were not my fault.

  Relief.

I did not want to come but I'm glad I did now.

Feel more comfortable. The group got me out of myself. Not so worried.

- **What was helpful?**

  I feel a lot better after the meetings. I was really worried about things before I came into the room. Feel better when I go out.

  To talk to strangers. Get their opinion. Getting to know how they think.

  Talking in confidence.

  Jacki, Rachel and others in the group.

- **Not helpful**

  Nothing. (4 responses)

- **Other things needed**

  Advice.

- **Helpful to other members**

  Everybody helped each other.

  Sympathy.

- **Things which could be changed/done differently**

  Nothing. (4 responses)

- **Other thoughts about the experience**

  I like the group because you can explain how you feel, and what's going on and we help each other.

Talking.

Get someone else's opinion/outlook.

- **Suggestions for future groups**

  Yes, it could be mixed as men hurt and have feelings too.

- **Frequency**

  Monthly for six months   4

- **Transport arrangements**

  Fetched. Taxi home.

  Fine, no problems. They make sure you get there and back home.

- **Location**

  Alright.

  Fine. No problems.

- **Meeting room**

  Fine.

- **Refreshments**

  No complaints.

- **Usefulness** (Score: 1 – not at all; 10 – very useful)

  Four respondents:

  8

  10

I would like to say 10 because it's helped me to realise that what happened to me wasn't my fault, and I haven't tried to hurt myself since attending my group.

Very useful 10.

Concluding remarks

There are some advantages when evaluation questionnaires can be anonymised, as people may be more honest about their thoughts if they know they are not going to be identified. It was impossible to ensure this in the Beyond Existing groups as we could recognise handwriting, or questionnaires were returned from residential homes – so identifying the member. Undertaking these written evaluations did indicate to us that the support we were providing was valued by most members. There were no specific suggestions about how we could do things differently. Rachel and I felt that members were honest with us when we had verbal evaluations during the sessions; we learnt what the members found helpful and how they wanted to work in future sessions.

CHAPTER 11

Conclusion

Beyond Existing was set up in order to test out whether groupwork could offer older people who had been abused the support they required in order to meet their needs – needs being defined as those resulting from past or current abuse. Three groups were run in a two-year period to test out different ways of working. The main conclusion is that groupwork can be an effective way of providing help (in the broadest sense) to victims of abuse, but that this method of working might not suit everyone, or that it could be combined with other ways of working. In this final chapter, I draw some conclusions about Beyond Existing, which may be of use to other workers who might be considering using groupwork to provide long-term support to vulnerable adults who have suffered abuse earlier in life or more recently.

Benefits of groupwork for victims

The whole subject of abuse is a very emotive issue and one might think that reading about it could be depressing; I hope this book has proved to the reader that this need not be the case. The work undertaken through Beyond Existing shows that much can be achieved and that there are reasons for optimism. I frequently hear comments from workers that 'nothing can be done' to help victims of adult abuse; there seems to be an implicit attitude that older people in particular do not have the capacity to change, or that if victims have lived in an abusive situation for a long time, they are unlikely to leave it. Having such attitudes is dangerous and does not promote good or creative practice with victims.

Victims may choose to deal with abuse and related unresolved issues at different times in their lives; every victim must be treated as an individual and helping must be adapted in response to that individuality. Workers should not assume that every victim is going to respond in a similar way. Consequently, the long-term work which needs to be done with a victim may in some cases last for a considerable length of time. At a time when the care management system restricts many social workers in the adult sector to undertaking assessments, and limits their long-term involvement and their professional use of imaginative methods of working, it is important that other workers (from all disciplines) become complementarily involved so that their skills can be utilised to support and help victims to achieve healing in the long term.

The findings from the Beyond Existing project support the findings of the original research project; namely, that victims *do* want to talk about their abusive experiences and that they may have an ongoing need for practical advice, information and support. The original interviewees had said that they would like to meet other victims and this was the primary reason for setting up Beyond Existing – that is, to test out whether and how groupwork could be advantageous. It has been evident that the victims who became members of the Beyond Existing groups found it very beneficial to meet with each other – not only to share their experiences and work towards healing, but also to help and support each other with past and current problems (not only those directly related to the outcomes of abuse). This validates Doel and Sawdon's comment about the rewards of groupwork: '...the value of reciprocity, both the giving and the receiving of help' (Doel and Sawdon 1999, p.24). In preceding chapters I have described how some members formed close bonds with each other, and also how some took a lead in sessions and acted as role models. Having the experience of abuse in common, and because of the relationships they formed in the groups, members were better able to understand and influence each other.

Looking forward

Although much of the work done in the groups focused on what had happened to members in the past, one very positive achievement for them was that they looked to the future with hope. Many members had experienced the most horrendous types of abuse and some had lived in those situations for most of their lives. Yet their strengths lay in their faith that the future could hold something better for them. This could be linked to the fact that many of them held religious beliefs; they were not only looking towards death and the after-life, but were optimistic also for the immediate foreseeable future. Another striking feature of members' attitudes was that they harboured virtually no bitterness about what had happened to them, rather a philosophical acceptance of their suffering.

Meeting needs

The original research project highlighted that victims of abuse will have many different types of need relating both to the past and the present (Pritchard 2000, 2001). The key needs which were met by the Beyond Existing groups were as follows. It will be apparent that these needs fall into three types: the expression and acceptance of feelings and events; discovering/maintaining a sense of direction in their lives; and day-to-day practical matters.

Feelings and events in the past

- to meet other victims and share with them

- to be believed/understood

- to talk about abuse – recent and past

- to vent anger and frustration and to come to terms with these feelings

- to build self-esteem and confidence.

Seeking a sense of direction

- to reminisce

- to undertake a life review

- to face up to the future, including, in some instances, their own death.

Practical problems

- information about residential care and the choices available to them

- alternative accommodation when the current situation remains painful

- how to get a bus pass, and other entitlements

- information about the legal system – e.g. restraining orders, rights and responsibilities

- information about health issues, particularly the problems of excessive alcohol use

- to plan for the future in a spirit of independence, avoiding the fears, collusions and panics of the past.

Changes

When reflecting back on what has been achieved, one finds evidence that, through groupwork, members were able to change their attitudes, feelings and behaviours. Many victims (and certainly most members of Beyond Existing) often blame themselves for the abuse they have suffered. A major achievement in all the groups was that members no longer blamed themselves, but came to understand more about the role adopted by their abusers and the pressures which led to it, both within themselves and in the abusers. Rachel and I felt our greatest achievement was to help members recognise and acknowledge their own strengths. They very often saw themselves as 'weak' and were seriously lacking in self-esteem. By giving them the opportunity to talk about what they had achieved in their lives and what they could still do, they were shown just how courageous and strong they really were. Where they needed to develop skills, particularly in relation to becoming more assertive in certain situations, the groupwork methods made this achievable.

Combining methods of working

So far I have been putting forward arguments regarding the advantages of undertaking groupwork. It must be acknowledged that groupwork might not be a suitable method of work for every victim. Some will need to work on a one-to-one basis because they feel uncomfortable talking and/or sharing experiences in a group setting. This was particularly so in the early stages of meeting, and occasionally recurred. Some victims needed a combination of methods; that is, attending a group and yet still having a one-to-one relationship with another worker outside the group, who undertook work specifically on the issues of abuse and healing. It is imperative in these situations that the group leaders and individual workers liaise closely with one another, and that the victim agrees to this sharing of information.

It is necessary to remember that most abusive situations entail an ambivalence of feelings in the victim. Some people control their ambivalence by splitting the positive and negative components and attributing them to the 'excellence' or 'uselessness' of their helpers. Hence the need for agreements about liaison. Life is difficult enough without the hazards of uncontrolled transference and countertransference!

Running support groups for abused adults

The practical problems encountered in setting up and running the Beyond Existing groups have been discussed in detail throughout the book (see Table 11.1 for a list of the basic requirements). In conclusion I can say that, although a lot of time is required in organising groupwork, it was found to be a beneficial way of working with victims of abuse and one which can be undertaken cost-effectively – that is, with a small budget and with reliance more on human than on financial resources.

Much has already been said about the value of bringing victims together, but we must also consider the role of the leaders in this type of groupwork (see Table 11.2 for skills and qualities needed). The members did support and help each other; so the leaders' main responsibility was to facilitate the smooth running of the sessions and, crucially, to provide a

Table 11.1 Basic requirements for running a group
• commitment
• people to give advice/support to leaders
• time
• skilled group leaders
• knowledge and understanding about abuse
• venue
• transport
• refreshments

therapeutic environment. By 'therapeutic', I refer to a setting which feels safe, unthreatening, unhurried and accepting. This can only be achieved when a leader has knowledge and understanding about abuse (that is, child abuse, domestic violence and adult abuse); for without this expertise and the necessary skills that expertise engenders, a leader cannot undertake methods of working which aim to work through the healing process. A leader has to be prepared to handle disclosure, and be able to provide the appropriate responses; otherwise a member could be dangerously harmed emotionally. I think, for example, of the dangers of presupposing how a victim is feeling, making assumptions about how s/he should respond, and – in effect – compelling the construction of emotional untruths. The leader has to be able to support a member in reliving the abuse, dealing with and understanding it in the victim's own terms, and developing the victim's own strategies to heal the damage.

Table 11.2 Skills and qualities needed by a leader
• listening
• observational
• analytical (i.e. understanding why things are being said or done in a particular mode/format)
• knowledge
• expertise in, and the appropriate application of, relationship skills
• understanding (both of the other person and of one's own preoccupations, biases, etc.)
• empathy
• support
• warmth
• trustworthiness
• communication
• patience
• making people feel safe/comfortable
• encouraging participation
• controlling your own emotions
• being able to detach oneself/cut off, particularly when a session has ended and evaluation begins

Creative working

The Beyond Existing project was fortunate in that different ways of working could be tested out; we were able to work creatively and try things which might have seemed rather revolutionary. What has been proved is that victims of abuse, regardless of age and gender, can work together productively in a group, and that those who initially present different problems or disabilities can also benefit from meeting in a group situation and working to help each other, as well as themselves. In short, the message to workers is that they must not be blinkered in their approach to working with vulnerable adults. In a time when resources are tight, managers at a senior level, as well as practitioners, must look across specialisms and pool resources and expertise, not only the resources and expertise of workers, but also those of the service users. Beyond Existing has demonstrated that much can be gained from bringing service users together from different specialisms – older people, mental health, learning disability.

Recommendations

In the future, organisations working with vulnerable adults should look to the opportunities of developing groups to support adults who have been abused, whether in childhood or adulthood or both (see Table 11.3 for the key groupwork findings). Groupwork is beneficial not only to the victim of abuse but also to the organisation and its workers. In practical terms it can be cost-effective; and, what is more important, it can be an extremely rewarding way of working – both for members and leaders.

Table 11.3 Summary of key findings for groupwork with abused adults
• Groups can be run with a small budget.
• Leaders need knowledge and understanding about child abuse, domestic violence and adult abuse.
• Male and female victims can work together in one group.
• Younger and older adults can work together in one group.
• Victims of abuse will have some common needs (e.g. the need to talk about their experiences), but individual needs must also be acknowledged.
• Leaders need to create a climate in which members feel they can express their difficulties with other members (or the leaders).

The future for Beyond Existing

At the time of writing the Morrison Group continues to meet on a monthly basis. In the past month two new members have been referred. One woman in her 60s has attended one session and believes the group will be able to help her to face the abuse she experienced in her childhood; she wants help to be able to tell her mother what happened to her. The other new member is in her 30s and has also experienced child sexual abuse; she has fears for her daughter, who is approaching the age when she herself suffered abuse. We also have male victims who have placed themselves on a waiting list for a group to begin, but that will depend on funding being secured. It is to be hoped that we can continue the positive work which has been started through Beyond Existing, and that other organisations will re-cognise a moral responsibility to help and support victims of abuse towards a long-term resolution of suffering. Dealing efficiently with crises as they happen is essential, but it is not enough.

Appendices

Poster for Victims

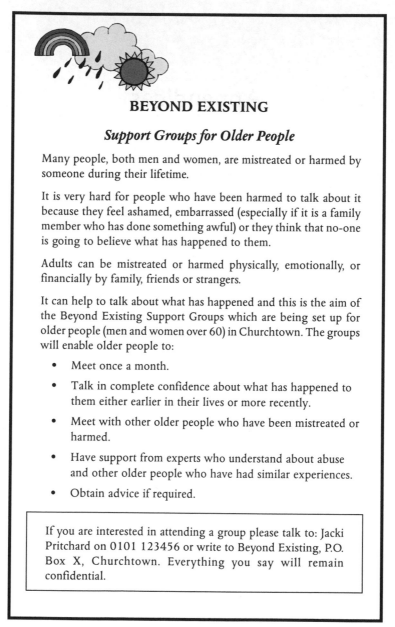

BEYOND EXISTING

Support Groups for Older People

Many people, both men and women, are mistreated or harmed by someone during their lifetime.

It is very hard for people who have been harmed to talk about it because they feel ashamed, embarrassed (especially if it is a family member who has done something awful) or they think that no-one is going to believe what has happened to them.

Adults can be mistreated or harmed physically, emotionally, or financially by family, friends or strangers.

It can help to talk about what has happened and this is the aim of the Beyond Existing Support Groups which are being set up for older people (men and women over 60) in Churchtown. The groups will enable older people to:

- Meet once a month.

- Talk in complete confidence about what has happened to them either earlier in their lives or more recently.

- Meet with other older people who have been mistreated or harmed.

- Have support from experts who understand about abuse and other older people who have had similar experiences.

- Obtain advice if required.

> If you are interested in attending a group please talk to: Jacki Pritchard on 0101 123456 or write to Beyond Existing, P.O. Box X, Churchtown. Everything you say will remain confidential.

Poster for Professionals, Workers and Others

BEYOND EXISTING

Support Groups for Older People Who Have Been Abused

DO YOU KNOW OR SUSPECT THAT AN OLDER PERSON IS BEING ABUSED
…in the past or now?

For more information about support groups being run for victims of abuse in Churchtown contact:

Telephone: 0101 123456
or write to:
Beyond Existing,
P.O. Box X,
Churchtown

SAFETY AND PRIVACY WILL BE RESPECTED

Leaflets for Victims

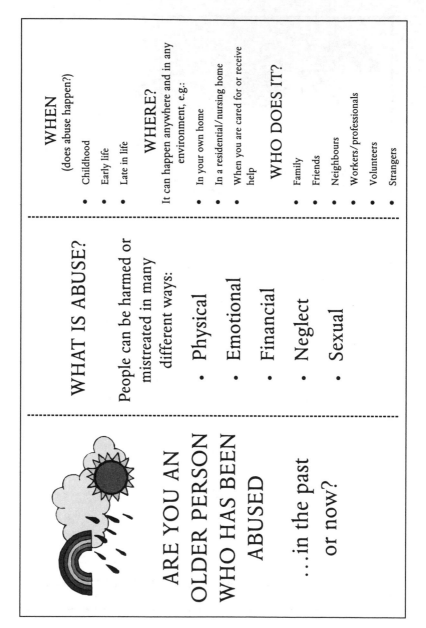

WHEN
(does abuse happen?)

- Childhood
- Early life
- Late in life

WHERE?
It can happen anywhere and in any environment, e.g.:

- In your own home
- In a residential/nursing home
- When you are cared for or receive help

WHO DOES IT?

- Family
- Friends
- Neighbours
- Workers/professionals
- Volunteers
- Strangers

WHAT IS ABUSE?

People can be harmed or mistreated in many different ways:

- Physical
- Emotional
- Financial
- Neglect
- Sexual

ARE YOU AN OLDER PERSON WHO HAS BEEN ABUSED

...in the past or now?

BEYOND EXISTING
SUPPORT GROUPS FOR OLDER PEOPLE WHO HAVE BEEN ABUSED

Many people, both men and women, are mistreated or harmed by someone during their lifetime.

It is very hard for people who have been harmed to talk about it because they might feel ashamed, embarrassed or think that no-one is going to believe what has happened to them.

It can help to talk about what has happened.

Two support groups have been set up in Churchtown.

The groups meet once a month *in a safe environment* so that people can:

- talk in confidence about what has happened to them

- meet with other people who have been mistreated or harmed

- have support from experts who understand about abuse.

TRANSPORT CAN BE ARRANGED TO GET YOU TO A GROUP MEETING

WHAT ARE THE GROUPS LIKE?

Older people who have regularly attended the Beyond Existing Groups have said:

'You get introduced to everyone and everyone gets to know you'

'You can talk in here. Nowhere else will they listen to you'

'You've always got someone to back you up'

'I feel very comfortable and safe in this group'

'I've gained knowledge'

'Nice people – that makes a difference'

CONTACT DETAILS

If you would like more information about attending one of the groups you can:

Telephone: 0101 123456

or

Write to:

Beyond Existing
P.O. Box X
Churchtown

SAFETY AND PRIVACY WILL BE RESPECTED

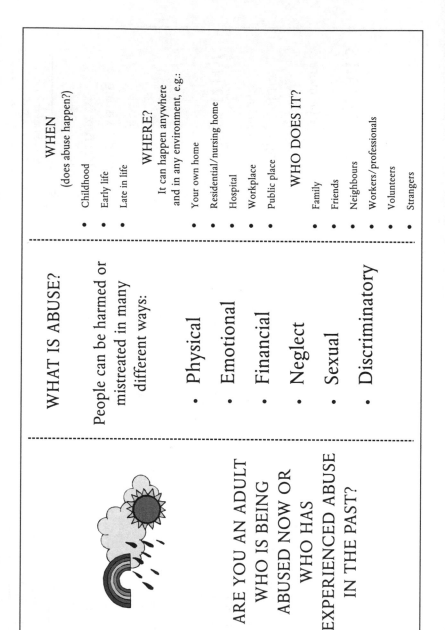

WHEN
(does abuse happen?)

- Childhood
- Early life
- Late in life

WHERE?

It can happen anywhere
and in any environment, e.g.:

- Your own home
- Residential/nursing home
- Hospital
- Workplace
- Public place

WHO DOES IT?

- Family
- Friends
- Neighbours
- Workers/professionals
- Volunteers
- Strangers

WHAT IS ABUSE?

People can be harmed or
mistreated in many
different ways:

- Physical
- Emotional
- Financial
- Neglect
- Sexual
- Discriminatory

ARE YOU AN ADULT
WHO IS BEING
ABUSED NOW OR
WHO HAS
EXPERIENCED ABUSE
IN THE PAST?

BEYOND EXISTING

SUPPORT GROUPS FOR ADULTS
WHO HAVE BEEN ABUSED

Many people, both men and women, are mistreated or harmed by someone during their lifetime.

It is very hard for people who have been harmed to talk about it because they might feel ashamed, embarrassed or think that no-one is going to believe what has happened to them. It can help to talk about what has happened.

Support groups have been running for over two years now in the Churchtown area.

The groups meet once a month *in a safe environment* so that people can:

- talk in confidence about what has happened to them
- meet with other people who have been mistreated or harmed
- obtain practical advice and support from experts who understand about abuse
- work through their feelings regarding the abuse they have experienced.

WHAT ARE THE GROUPS LIKE?

Adults who have regularly attended the Beyond Existing Groups have said:

'You get introduced to everyone and everyone gets to know you'

'You can talk in here. Nowhere else will they listen to you'

'You've always got someone to back you up'

'I feel very comfortable and safe in this group'

'A strength is being able to share with others'

'I've gained knowledge'

'Being a survivor means you see things for what they really are'

'Nice people – that makes a difference'

CONTACT DETAILS

If you would like more information about attending a group you can:

Telephone: 0101 123456

or

Write to:

Beyond Existing
P.O. Box X
Churchtown

SAFETY AND PRIVACY WILL BE RESPECTED

Leaflet for Professionals, Workers and Others

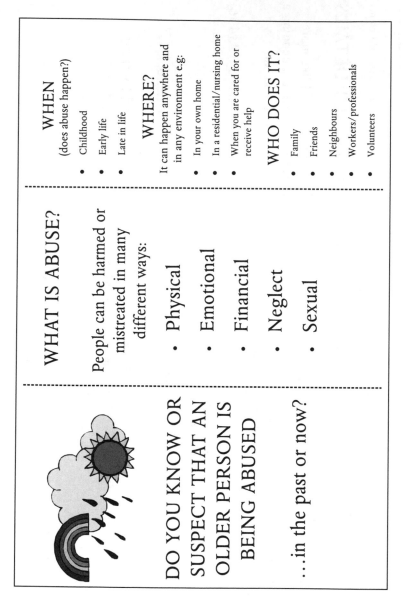

WHAT IS ABUSE?

People can be harmed or mistreated in many different ways:

- Physical
- Emotional
- Financial
- Neglect
- Sexual

WHEN
(does abuse happen?)

- Childhood
- Early life
- Late in life

WHERE?

It can happen anywhere and in any environment e.g:

- In your own home
- In a residential/nursing home
- When you are cared for or receive help

WHO DOES IT?

- Family
- Friends
- Neighbours
- Workers/professionals
- Volunteers

DO YOU KNOW OR SUSPECT THAT AN OLDER PERSON IS BEING ABUSED

…in the past or now?

BEYOND EXISTING

SUPPORT GROUPS FOR OLDER PEOPLE WHO HAVE BEEN ABUSED

Many people, both men and women, are mistreated or harmed by someone during their lifetime.

It is very hard for people who have been harmed to talk about it because they might feel ashamed, embarrassed or think that no-one is going to believe what has happened to them.

It can help to talk about what has happened.

Two support groups have been set up in Churchtown.

The groups meet once a month *in a safe environment* so that people can:

- talk in confidence about what has happened to them
- meet with other people who have been mistreated or harmed
- have support from experts who understand about abuse.

> TRANSPORT CAN BE ARRANGED TO GET OLDER PEOPLE TO A GROUP MEETING

WHAT ARE THE GROUPS LIKE?

Older people who have regularly attended the Beyond Existing Groups have said:

'You get introduced to everyone and everyone gets to know you'

'You can talk in here. Nowhere else will they listen to you'

'You've always got someone to back you up'

'I feel very comfortable and safe in this group'

'I've gained knowledge'

'Nice people – that makes a difference'

CONTACT DETAILS

If you would like more information about attending a group you can:

Telephone: 0101 123456

or

Write to:

Beyond Existing
P.O. Box X
Churchtown

> SAFETY AND PRIVACY WILL BE RESPECTED

References

Bass, E. and Davis, L. (1988) *The Courage to Heal.* New York: Harper and Row.

Bernard, L., Burton, J., Kyne, P. and Simon, J. (1988) 'Groups for Older People in Residential and Day Care: The Other Groupworkers.' *Groupwork 1,* 2, 115–123.

Brown, A. (1994) *Groupwork,* 3rd edition. Aldershot: Ashgate.

Burton, J. (1989) 'Institutional Change and Group Action: The Significance and Influence of Groups in Developing New Residential Services for Older People.' In A. Brown and R. Clough (eds) *Groups and Groupings: Life and Work in Day and Residential Centres.* London: Tavistock/Routledge.

Crimmens, P. (1998) *Storymaking and Creative Groupwork with Older People.* London: Jessica Kingsley Publishers.

Davies, B. (1975) *The Use of Groups in Social Work Practice.* London: Routledge and Kegan Paul.

Department of Health (1993) *No Longer Afraid: The Safeguard of Older People in Domestic Settings.* London: HMSO.

Department of Health (2000) *No Secrets: Guidance on Developing and Implementing Multi-Agency Policies and Procedures to Protect Vulnerable Adults from Abuse.* London: HMSO.

Doel, M. and Sawdon, C. (1999) *The Essential Groupworker: Teaching and Learning Creative Groupwork.* London: Jessica Kingsley Publishers.

Douglas, T (2000) *Basic Groupwork,* 2nd edition. London: Routledge.

Gillies, C. and James, A. (1994) *Reminiscence Work with Old People.* London: Chapman and Hall.

Gordy, P. L. (1983) 'Group Work that Supports Adult Victims of Childhood Incest.' *Social Casework 64,* 300–307.

Hall, L. and Lloyd, S. (1989) *Surviving Child Sexual Abuse.* London: Falmer Press.

Heap, K. (1979) *Process and Action in Work with Groups.* Oxford: Pergamon.

Heap, K. (1985) *The Practice of Social Work with Groups: A Systematic Approach.* London: George Allen and Unwin.

Joseph Rowntree Foundation (May 2000) Findings: *The Needs of Older Women: Services for Victims of Elder Abuse and Other Abuse.* York: Joseph Rowntree Foundation.

Konopka, G. (1983) *Social Group Work: A Helping Process.* 3rd edition. Englewood Cliffs, NJ: Prentice-Hall.

Lewis, G. (1992) 'Groupwork in a Residential Home for Older People: Building on the Positive Aspects of Group Living.' *Groupwork 5,* 1, 50–57.

McCullough, M. K. and Ely, P. J. (1989) *Social Work with Groups.* London: Routledge.

Mullender, A. (1990) 'Groupwork in Residential Settings for Elderly People.' *Groupwork 3,* 3, 286–301.

Mullender, A. and Ward, D. (1991) *Self-Directed Groupwork: Users Take Action for Empowerment.* London: Whiting and Birch.

Phillips, J. (2001) *Groupwork in Social Care.* London: Jessica Kingsley Publishers.

Pritchard, J. (2000) *The Needs of Older Women: Services for Victims of Elder Abuse and Other Abuse.* Bristol: The Policy Press.

Pritchard, J. (2001) *Male Victims of Elder Abuse: Their Experiences and Needs.* London: Jessica Kingsley Publishers.

Sanderson, C. (1995) *Counselling Adult Survivors of Child Sexual Abuse,* 2nd edition. London: Jessica Kingsley Publishers.

Shulman, L. (1988) 'Groupwork Practice with Hard to Reach Clients: A Modality of Choice.' *Groupwork 1,* 1, 5–16.

Steinmetz, S. K. (1978) 'The Battered Husband Syndrome.' *Victimology 2,* 499–509.

Subject Index

incest survivors groups, 40
interruptions, preventing,
    73–74, 164

Jim, 48, 59, 109, 111, 119,
    128, 135
Joseph Rowntree Foundation,
    16, 20, 24, 28, 42
judgementalism, 120

Kathleen, 59–60, 113–14,
    131, 142, 170

leaders
    abuse history of, 31–32
    debriefing sessions for, 82,
        83, 159, 160, 161–62
    emotions of, 160–61
    gender of, 31, 168
    member relationships with,
        73
    one versus two, 84, 161–62
    skills and qualities needed,
        158–59, 197–99
    supervision for, 83, 159, 160
    transport provided by, 73,
        75, 166
    use of term, 8
life reviews
    bereavement, 126–28
    depression, 130–31
    early life, 124–26
    loss, 129
    previous relationships, 126
    regrets, 126
Lilian, 36, 47, 48, 60–61, 73,
    75, 79, 80–81, 99–100,
    105, 109, 110–11,

116–18, 119–20, 125,
    127–28, 132, 141,
    164–65, 169, 172, 174,
    178, 179
literacy problems, 43, 65, 100
loneliness, 129–30, 148–49
long-term work
    lack of resources for, 10–11
    need for, 23–24, 193
    and open groups, 39–41
loss, 127–29
    see also bereavement

males, sexual abuse of, 21, 22,
    111
Marjorie, 39, 62, 78, 81,
    95–96, 100, 111, 126,
    129–30, 130–31,
    131–32, 133, 134–35,
    136, 140, 142, 183
medical conditions, support for,
    136, 170
meetings see sessions
members
    as abusers, 52
    age range of, 69–70
    new, in open groups, 40
    types of abuse experienced,
        51, 52
    use of term, 8
    vignettes of, 53–69
methods, of groupwork
    combining, 196–97
    new ideas, trying out, 89–90
    preference for traditional, 89
Morrison group, 25, 38, 39,
    81, 84, 88–89, 90, 92,
    100, 101, 169, 170, 174,
    201
multiple victims, 54, 114

Author Index